THERE IS NO APP FOR
HAPPINESS

THERE IS NO APP FOR
HAPPINESS

HOW TO AVOID
A NEAR-LIFE EXPERIENCE

MAX STROM

Skyhorse Publishing

Skyhorse Publishing books may be purchased in bulk at special discounts for sales promotion, corporate gifts, fund-raising, or educational purposes. Special editions can also be created to specifications. For details, contact the Special Sales Department, Skyhorse Publishing, 307 West 36th Street, 11th Floor, New York, NY 10018 or info@skyhorsepublishing.com.

Skyhorse® and Skyhorse Publishing® are registered trademarks of Skyhorse Publishing, Inc.®, a Delaware corporation.

www.skyhorsepublishing.com

10 9 8 7 6 5 4 3 2 1

Library of Congress Cataloging-in-Publication Data is available on file.

ISBN 978-1-62087-636-7

Printed in the United States of America

Consult a licensed medical professional before beginning any practice related to health or exercise. Should you choose to make use of the information contained herein without first consulting a health professional, you are prescribing for yourself, which is your right. The author and publisher do not assume any responsibility whatsoever under any conditions or circumstances.

CONTENTS

ACKNOWLEDGMENTS

I extend my sincere thanks to:

My editor Jenn McCartney for her belief in this book.

Tony Lyons for his support.

The great team at Skyhorse Publishing.

Andrea Barzvi at ICM for her strength and guidance.

Liz Delaney and Kristin Garbarino for their help with editing.

A special thanks to my friend Chris Silbermann.

And my deepest gratitude to my wife, Stephanie Cate Strom, for her insight and help with editing, her belief in me, and her dedication to the truth.

PART ONE:
THE WORLD WE LIVE IN NOW

HOW TO AVOID A NEAR-LIFE EXPERIENCE

We sometimes hear about near-death experiences from the news or even from someone we know and trust. These mysterious and powerful experiences usually involve a person being pronounced clinically dead for a few minutes but who is then brought back to life. It is fascinating, and for many of us reassuring to hear of the uncannily similar experiences of those who have gone through the beginning stages of dying and then returned to tell us that what they experienced was not pain or terror, but a sense of great peace and unconditional love. Many have an out of body experience, even observing a medical team performing resuscitation efforts on their lifeless body. Many describe a tunnel through which they move toward a powerful, clear, and beautiful light. Many claim to receive a rapid life review, *the life-flashing-before-your-eyes event*, while others even report receiving knowledge about the nature of life and the universe itself. Quite often, a powerful catharsis like these near-death experiences will cause a drastic readjustment in the person's life trajectory; he or she can be essentially reborn and will start a new life. In cases such as these, it seems that the closer to death we come, the more committed we are in choosing to live a fuller life after receiving a second chance.

What this book begins with is not extraordinary stories of near-death experiences, but a much more common phenomenon I call *a near-life experience*. This is when a person comes to the end of his life and looks back with abject regret from the recognition that his life could have been so much more, and with haunting realizations such as, *I could have, but didn't . . .* or *Why didn't I say I love you when I had the chance?* A near-life experience is to know that you had the opportunity for a rich and meaningful life but missed it because you instead chose, or resigned yourself to, something far less. A near-life experience could be the saddest tragedy of all because it is an avoidable one, because it is a result of our own choices.

This book is to help you determine if you are truly happy and, if not, to give you some tools to empower you to remove the obstacles that keep you from happiness. It will challenge you to understand how you define happiness and what it means to be a human being in a modern world. For a life truly and fully lived, you must be willing to let go of things that no longer serve you, and embrace new actions that empower you in the deepest possible ways. A journey like this begins with looking into the mirror and studying yourself—not meekly, but with the excitement of an archaeologist making a discovery—and learning to look outside your own box of social conditioning. This isn't easy, partly because most of us are so incredibly busy working long hours to get ahead, get out of debt, or just to stay afloat, or are exhausted from raising children, going to school, or putting our kids through school. And it is also challenging because we have to overcome our presets, the social programming that triggers behavior that is sometimes exactly the opposite of what we need or even want.

This book is going to illuminate the two most significant trends that are impacting your life, and then introduce you to the three most important actions you can take to look at your world with fresh eyes, overcome your negative presets, and propel yourself into a new and more meaningful experience of living.

While we have been busy with our hyperscheduled lives, we have quietly arrived at the threshold of a new era, the beginning of a new cultural paradigm unlike anything we have ever known. Yet too many of us haven't yet realized that we live in a very different world than we did twenty years ago, and we are so distracted that we have become unaware of what we are feeling and why we are feeling it.

There are two extreme trends occurring now that are massively impacting our society and causing tectonic changes in our culture.

Trend 1: Technology is exploding exponentially.
Trend 2: We are becoming less happy.

Technology has begun to distract and overwhelm us while many of us find ourselves suffering from a strange malnutrition, a malnourished emotional state. This is because technology has expanded at such a rate that nearly every aspect of our world has been affected—our economy, medical industry, manufacturing, military, and education, and especially how we interrelate with each other—and technological growth is now happening so fast that we live in an ever-changing environment, which allows us to become masters of nothing. Yet with the exponential growth of information technology, there has been no corresponding expansion of personal happiness. Instead we find our society depressed, anxious, sleep deprived, and overmedicated.

Although the technology revolution has been surging for some time, it has gone largely unnoticed beyond the excitement of upgraded smartphones, social networking, iPads, and dazzling special effects in films and video gaming. But currently, because the exponential growth curve* has become steeper, almost doubling every year, things are moving faster and faster. (Remember that Facebook did not exist eight years ago.) Now the media is beginning to notice that our over infatuation with social media is concurrent with our slipping into an isolated lifestyle and has begun reporting it, but it is far from headline news.

> *** Explanation of exponential growth:** If I gave you a dollar every day for thirty days, at the end of the month you would have collected thirty dollars from me. This is an example of linear growth. But with exponential growth, if I would give you one dollar on the first day, the next day it would double, so I would give you two dollars; on the next day four, then eight, and so on. At the end of the month, you would collect over one billion dollars. According to some preeminent futurists, technological advances are growing so fast, they have nearly reached this point of doubling every year.

We are starting to become aware of something happening all around us but are barely processing it. Perhaps because we are so attached to what used to be, our minds cannot see what is in front of us. Like the Aztecs, who, according to legend, couldn't recognize the European ships carrying the conquistadors, we do not seem to fathom how our own world has changed. Socially, in our attempt to be more connected, we have actually, in mass, taken two steps back by choosing to abandon personal conversations in preference for impersonal communication via text. We have quickly transformed into a distracted society focused on entertainment dispensed from flat screens. In our everyday lives the Information Age has really manifested as the Entertainment Age, and it appears that we are already having trouble deciphering the difference between life and entertainment. Yet with all this, many of us are not informed of just how vast the coming changes are. Here are two examples of extraordinary developments that experts predict are coming our way within twenty years.

Many scientists believe that increasing the average human life span to 150 years is well within reach in the near future, with most of those years being vital and productive. Some even assert that we will be able to reverse aging and that a 150-year lifespan is a conservative projection.[1]

And while you ponder the ramifications of an additional fifty or so years of healthy living, both personally and for society, consider the following . . .

Artificial intelligence (AI) experts predict that by around 2030 the common computer will not only surpass human level intelligence, but will become self-aware, meaning that it will develop human-like consciousness.[2]

These are not predictions from the basements of science fiction and comic book enthusiasts, but from many of the preeminent scientists in the fields of longevity and AI.

But once again, what we are not having, tragically, is exponential growth of happiness. In fact, there is a lot of talk about the nature of happiness lately because it is becoming increasingly elusive. Despite all of the wondrous marvels that have entered our lives, statistics show that we are far less happy than we were twenty years ago. It could be said that we are witnessing an emotional collapse of industrialized society. From New York to London to Beijing, in the richest societies of the world, we find ourselves depressed, anxious, and sleep deprived, with few solutions being offered other than medicating the symptoms. The overcomplexity

---

[1] "Living to 100 and Beyond." *New York Times* August 27, 2011

[2] *Transcendent Man* – 2009 documentary film by American filmmaker Barry Ptolemy

and ever-changing environment we find ourselves in cause anxiety and confusion, and a person continually confronted with massive change may withdraw into a more insular life in order to cope. We never planned to settle for a life of merely coping, yet we seem to have accepted it as inevitable, so we swallow our pills, becoming a society that now medicates our emotions, believing there are no other alternatives. This could be the cause of the alarming increase in suicides. Doctor Ian Rockett, professor in the West Virginia University School of Public Health, led a 2012 study that claims the suicide rate has increased fifteen percent in the last ten years and is now the leading cause of injury death in America—*ahead* of motor vehicle accidents.

Other statistics reveal that we are turning to pharmaceuticals in mass and have become a medicated society of unprecedented proportions. For example, one in four women in the United States takes antidepressants and/or antianxiety medication[3], with the men not far behind. And for sleep? About one in four adults takes medication every night, and these numbers are growing alarmingly fast. Taking medications is sometimes appropriate and doesn't mean someone is wrong for doing so, but what it often means is one has gone to a doctor and essentially said, "I am unhappy, I have run out of options, and I don't know what else to do."

Now, when we use the word *happiness*, what do we mean exactly? From my experience working with tens of thousands of students, most people have only a partial or vague notion of what brings them happiness, and they usually confuse it with pleasure, material wealth, and power. In this book, when I use the term *happiness*, I do not mean pleasure based on external circumstances, such as the perfect house, an exciting romance, or a glamorous holiday.

---

[3] From Medco Health Solutions report, Nov. 2011

We know now that happiness is not predicated primarily on external circumstances. There are poor people who are the most joyful you will ever meet, and there are people who are rich and famous yet are absolutely miserable. What I'm talking about is a meaningful life. I find that when people feel like they have meaning in their lives, they define themselves as happy. They want to get up in the morning and have something to live for that is larger than they are. Meaning brings fulfillment. I personally define happiness as *the daily experience of a meaningful life.*

So, we have an explosion of technology that is growing exponentially, yet simultaneously we have a decline in happiness in our culture. I believe these two trends are connected. I believe there is no app for happiness, that there is no software for a meaningful life, and that at the deepest levels of human fulfillment, we grossly overestimate what technology can do for us. For example, we all have smartphones now that perform tasks we wouldn't have dreamed possible twenty years ago, and we say they have improved our ability to communicate. We communicate constantly, this is true, but has your smartphone improved the *quality* of communication with your loved ones? Has your smartphone improved your relationships? Do you have more fulfilling conversations with your family on your smartphone?

To be clear, I am not anti technology; I do not live off the grid in a hay-bale house and grow all of my own food. On the contrary, I use a laptop, I use the Internet, I love my GPS, and I am grateful to have them. I am even an advocate of self-driving cars.[4] I am also in awe that millions of people who cannot afford to go to school can now access free education online from sources such as

---

[4] "Hands on the future: Transparent armor and a fully autonomous car" by Jason Hiner for Between the Lines, March 6, 2013

the Khan Academy[5] or University of the People.[6] And I am excited to know that in the near future, if a man discovers that he has heart disease, biomedicine will be able to grow him a new heart from his own cells to replace his sick one. This is all excellent use of new technology.

But will biomedicine repair a broken heart? Our basic emotional needs have not changed. There is even work being done to create human organs with 3D printers,[7] so perhaps we will one day be writing songs with lyrics like, "She broke my heart, so I printed a new one."

This is the key point: One problem can be fixed with science, and the other cannot. Technology will repair the blood pump but not a broken heart. A GPS will help us find our way through the city, but it will not help us find our way through our relationships. Biomedicine will add more years to our life, but will that mean an additional decade of anxiety and sleep deprivation?

Do you really believe—in your heart of hearts—that your chief personal problems with happiness, relationships, intimacy, or depression will be solved with better technology? Are you just waiting for the right app to come along?

What everyone wants is to be happy, fulfilled, connected to others, and brimming with purpose—and for this, I believe that technology is close to irrelevant. But we must be careful not to confuse a virtual world for an actual, vital world. Does an infant need a virtual mother? Does a drowning man need a virtual life preserver? Will a

---

[5] The Khan Academy is a non-profit educational website created in 2006 by American educator Salman Khan, a graduate of MIT and Harvard Business School.

[6] University of the People (UoPeople) is a non-profit, tuition-free, unaccredited online academic institution founded by entrepreneur Shai Reshef

[7] Anthony Atala is the director of the Wake Forest Institute for Regenerative Medicine, where his work focuses on growing and regenerating tissues and organs. His team engineered the first lab-grown organ to be implanted into a human—a bladder—and is developing experimental fabrication technology that can "print" human tissue on demand. – from TED.com

starving woman be fed with virtual food? No, of course not. So then why would a virtual friendship suffice? The answer is, it will not.

This extraordinary technological revolution as well as these unstable economic times challenge us to look at ourselves and determine how we now define happiness and what we believe we need to do, or stop doing, in order to experience it.

The answer to all this is accelerating our personal transformation. This means that instead of waiting for life to teach us lessons via a series of random, devastating, or traumatic events, (posttraumatic growth), we instead take intentional action that accelerates our evolution so that we become wiser faster. I believe we must move from the Entertainment Age to the Age of Wisdom. As a teacher of personal transformation, what I want to focus on with you is what we can do about it on a very personal basis, to decide, as philosopher and Holocaust survivor Viktor Frankl once said, to "live as if you were living a second time, and as though you had acted wrongly the first time."[8]

This book reveals an internal human technology capable of empowering the most meaningful areas of your life and leading you to deeper levels of happiness. You have all the apps you need in your mind, body, and emotional center. But you need to upload this knowledge and begin using it.

---

[8] *Man's Search for Meaning* (1946) is a book by Viktor E. Frankl.

THE NEW CAMBRIAN EXPLOSION

The Exponential Growth and Impact of Information Technology

About 580 million years ago, most organisms were composed of single cells. Over the following seventy or eighty million years (relatively short span in Earth history) the rate of evolution suddenly accelerated and began to resemble the plant and animal life of today. This event is called the Cambrian Explosion. Not unlike this ancient Cambrian Explosion, the industrialized world of today is experiencing what could be called the New Cambrian Explosion. A common example is that it took mankind 50,000 years before the first telephone was invented in the mid 1870s. It took only about 100 years, until 1983, for the mobile phone to become commercially available. Then as the exponential curve spiked, from 1990 to 2011, worldwide mobile phone subscriptions grew from 12.4 million to over 5.6 billion, reaching into the developing nations and the bottom of the economic pyramid. As of 2011, about seventy percent of the world's population use mobile phones. Yet even with this significant acceptance of technology as a way of life, many of us have no idea how incredibly different things are with respect to biotechnology, computing, and robotics—even compared to twenty years ago.

Not unlike the Cambrian Explosion, when growth and development of organic life suddenly accelerated into living organisms in a relatively short period of time, information technology is accelerating exponentially and in the next twenty to thirty years will dramatically change much of our daily life.

Here are a few more examples of recent radical breakthroughs.

- Iris-scanning technology can now capture and identify your iris from thirty feet away even if you are running and wearing a mask and sunglasses. This is *today*, and it is likely that iris-scanning identification will replace our credit cards, passports, drivers licenses, pin codes, passwords, etc., within a decade.[9]
- Biotech scientists have already begun growing custom-made internal organs, beginning with the human bladder, in order to replace failing organs in patients.
- Google already has successfully developed a fully autonomous vehicle, a self-driving car that has traveled throughout the United States. Nissan's prototype will drop you off at a store and find its own parking space. Fully autonomous vehicles, or self-driving cars, are expected to be commercially available from several companies by around 2020. As of the publishing of this book, three states in the United States have already signed bills allowing self-driving cars on the streets, bringing this new technology into reality.
- Honda has demonstrated to the world a humanoid robot that can run, walk backwards, and pour a glass

---

[9] Jeff Carter – from TEDx Kansas City August 2012

of orange juice with the purpose of, among other applications, creating helpers for the elderly and physically challenged.

- But most astonishingly, as mentioned earlier, many of the world's top thinkers predict that the common laptop computer will be self-aware by around 2030. This isn't just a guess by homebound tech enthusiasts but by esteemed experts in the field of AI, who are predicting this with near certainty. That means your computer will have a mind similar to a human's. This will not just mean the ability to do arithmetic very quickly (it already does that now) but empowered with creative thought. It will have emotional intelligence and the capability of making ethical decisions. It will have creative capacities and skills such as writing books, designing, or making intelligent conversation. It will even have a sense of humor. And then as it continues to grow more intelligent, by 2035 or so, it will greatly surpass our intelligence.

To quote futurist and inventor Ray Kurzweil,

"Technological change is exponential, contrary to the common-sense, intuitive, linear view. So, we won't experience 100 years of progress in the 21st century, it will be more like 20,000 years of progress (at today's rate)."

I am convinced that the many facets of this New Cambrian Explosion will help us in many positive and profound ways. For example, our physical health will be enhanced, and our life span extended. Already, blood cell-sized submarines called nanobots are being tested. These will be used, among other tasks, to destroy tumors, unblock clots, and perform surgeries.

We will see the eradication of genetic diseases that cause great suffering, and we will benefit from the eventual repair or replacement of nonfunctioning ears and eyes, and even in helping those with spinal damage to regain control of their limbs.

The New Cambrian Explosion will be positive as self-driving cars[10] could eventually bring about the end of the annual massacre of over 40,000 people in the United States alone, as well as preventing 1.5 million injuries yearly. Our reliance on automobiles is, in my view, the deadliest human tragedy in the United States—an absurdly archaic system that careens forward daily without opposition.

And the New Cambrian Explosion will bring forth the improvement of the environment on several levels through increased production of food simultaneously with a decrease in the use of pesticides and petroleum fertilizers, and utilization of new, clean, and affordable energy. Solving the energy problem will be an immeasurably important development as it is, in my opinion, the industrial world's number two apex problem (number one is ethics). Clean and affordable energy will be the golden key to ending several global crises. It means that we will be able to convert seawater into fresh water, ending the world's water shortage. Clean and affordable energy will lead to massive reduction in the pollution of our biosphere and could, if implemented in time, help reduce the effects of global warming.

But the negatives of this Cambrian phenomenon are also potentially immense and likely to create new and unintended consequences as well, and this is because human ethics and compassion are not having a Cambrian explosion—not even a Cambrian sputter. It doesn't matter what we invent in the twenty-first century if our utilization of those inventions is based on primeval motivations. For every scientific breakthrough that

---

[10] "Green Light For Google's Driverless Car As It Receives First Autonomous License" by Peter Murray

can heal people or the planet itself, there are plenty of unethical people, people who are in complete disassociation with their conscience, who will take those innovations and use them for selfish intentions regardless of potential or direct harm to others. As Viktor Frankl so astutely proclaimed, "Since Auschwitz we know what man is capable of. And since Hiroshima we know what is at stake."

Here is a recent example: Despite the amazing developments in science, as you know, in 2008 the world economy collapsed. The collapse was not caused by a software glitch or problem that better technology could have solved, and it was not caused by stupid people; it was caused by people with high IQs and Ivy League educations—but who lacked ethics. (There is no app for ethics either.) We have enough technology to create a near-utopian world right now, but one thing stands in our way: ourselves. We still don't seem to know how to behave with kindness and cooperation for the good of all.

What kind of society are we? Conquering territories—power struggles—human exploitation . . . We live in an age in which we claim that we are more connected than we ever have been, but there are still human beings who capture, enslave, and smuggle children across borders to be sold as sex slaves. And the nations where these child sex slaves are smuggled into are the nations that commonly refer to themselves First World nations, the great centers of civilization.

No matter how advanced our technology becomes, we still function from the most primitive part of us, the reptilian brain. The thought process goes something like this: An early human ancestor would spot an unidentified object, and his reptilian brain would rapidly evaluate the object with a few simple survival questions.

1. Should I run from it or kill it?

If deemed safe, then further investigation is in order.

2. Can I eat it?
3. Can I mate with it?

Once the brain developed further, we began to determine if an object had other potential uses and added a fourth question.

4. Can I use it as a tool to kill?

And later, in more modern times, a fifth question:

5. Can I make money with it?

And only through evolved self-awareness does a human begin to consider if an object has purposes such as healing or benefiting humanity in general.

Going back to the reptilian mind's first three questions, consider these contemporary examples of the reptilian mind at work in the Information Age.

Question: What entity financed the development of the Internet?

Answer: The United States Defense Department. (Can I use it as a tool to kill?)

Question: What is the biggest money making business on the Internet?

Answer: Pornography. (Can I mate with it?)

Question: The current robotic revolution is being financed primarily by what entity?

Answer: Again, the United States Defense Department. (Can I kill with it?)

And Pleasure Bots, robots for sexual relations, are already fully in development in the private sector.

No matter how sophisticated one makes a machine, the inventor cannot determine the ultimate outcome of his or her invention. Though an intention may be altruistic, the intention may ultimately be irrelevant to the outcome. Just consider Brazilian aviation inventor, Alberto Santos-Dumont.

Santos-Dumont lived in Paris in the late 1800s and early 1900s and was able to finance his inventions from his inherited fortune. He was known for his innovative genius, but also for his generosity and kindness. Santos won a prestigious award and world notoriety for developing the preeminent bicycle-propelled balloon. Sometimes he would take a ride in his balloon, gliding along Paris boulevards at rooftop level, and land in front of Maxim's to have lunch. Later, he designed, built, and flew the first powered airplane in Europe. His first public flight was in Paris in 1906. Santos believed that the airplane would be a significant aid to advancing civilization. He didn't care about patenting his invention; in fact, he published the plans to his monoplane in 1910 in the *Popular Mechanics* magazine, which affirmed that his design was better than any other aircraft that had been built to date. Santos was so enthusiastic about aviation that he boldly and generously released the drawings of his plane for free in major newspapers in cities across the globe, (what we today call *open sourcing*) hoping that he could help launch a new prosperous era for mankind with aviation. That was his intention. But as soon as his plans reached the hands of the leading nations, they began to utilize his invention to create aerial war machines. World War I was the first war to use airplanes as weapons. This was so heartbreaking to Santos that it was one of the main causes that led to his suicide.

Albert Einstein lamented about his own contribution to the creation of the atomic bomb as is indicated in this sobering quote: "The release of atom power has changed everything except our way of thinking . . . the solution to this problem lies in the heart of mankind. If only I had known, I should have become a watchmaker."

The entire collapse of the world economy in 2008 was rooted in bad behavior, not bad technology. So why would we expect technology to solve the fundamental problems with human life if the problems are caused by lack of compassion or ethics? What technology will solve this? Even hyperrational scientists, futurists, and inventors succumb to the most irrational of feelings, compulsions, depression, sleep disorders, and resentment. I have met many people with impressive intellects and careers who are also admittedly addicted to antidepressants, sleep aids, and blood pressure medications because they have not learned the basic principles of happiness and health.

So, even though I am a hopeful supporter of the Information Age and an admirer of the many genius technophilanthropists who are working tirelessly to solve the world's crises, I do not believe that the Information Age, with all of its gifts and good intentions, will save us from our core issues, the fundamental human problems that encage us. It has become glaringly obvious that to transform and heal the world collectively, we must transform and heal ourselves individually.

DEFINING HAPPINESS

To seek happiness, it is crucial that you know what it is. It means that you must define it for yourself. If you've read *Alice in Wonderland*, perhaps you remember Alice asking the Cheshire Cat,

"Would you tell me, please, which way I ought to go from here?"

"That depends a good deal on where you want to get to," said the Cat.

"I don't much care where," said Alice.

"Then it doesn't matter which way you go," said the Cat.

Similarly, if you don't know what makes you happy, then it doesn't matter much what you do.

Wives and mothers can be especially challenged by such a question as how to define happiness. This is because quite often they haven't considered what truly makes them happy for years as they are constantly caring and tending to their family.

Many people live as if happiness is a commodity to be bought, or stolen. Some struggle in vain to find happiness through the shopping for and acquisition of clothing, electronics, and a new car. But eventually we discover that this is fruitless. Others define happiness as the experience of obtaining a goal such as finding a better job, getting married, having a child, or going on a really exciting adventure. These could all be classified as *peak happiness events*. But these peak events do not indicate someone will have a happy life when day-to-day existence sets in. Many people who are depressed are married, have children, have a good job, and take great vacations.

So, are most of the things we think we need to be happy actually relevant to happiness? Were there happy people before gadgets and machines? It is easy to forget that the men who propagated "Life, Liberty and the pursuit of Happiness" did not have electricity or flush toilets. The advent of electricity and indoor plumbing had not happened yet. In fact, it was not until Teddy Roosevelt's presidency that indoor plumbing began to arrive in the White House along with a single telephone line. Our founding fathers (and mothers) had no notion of an electrical world of machines, yet happiness was evidently quite attainable to them. However, today, upon permanently losing electricity, many of us would react as if it were the end of days. But if people were able to find happiness throughout the entire history of the world up until 100 or so years ago, without these devices and machines, perhaps we can too. My assertion is not to get rid of machines and electrical devices but to find happiness regardless of having them or not having them.

There is much that we think we need but actually only desire as a result of a deep craving and yearning to fill an emptiness inside or to cover and numb a pain within. Many of us are what I call *trapped in paradise*. But what if paradise is found on the inside?

Olga

Studies have shown that happiness is not predicated on external circumstances or objects. Science is now backing up what many of the great philosophers have been teaching for centuries, but it seems that even armed with this knowledge, it takes root in each of us at different times in our evolution.

There was a time in my life when I was inspired, as well as consumed, by the film world and worked as a screenwriter in Los Angeles. It was such an amazing and alluring subculture, where through this magical artistic medium one could potentially, in a short amount of time, achieve wealth, power, and fame, as well as meet smart, beautiful people to date. I remember a particular party in my home where I had a moment to myself, and I just looked around the room at my friends. It was then that I realized that nearly all of my friends were in the movie business: directors, actors, producers, writers, models, and stuntmen—an array of beautifully fit and charming people. Even glamorous. This was my new society. But as I looked closely at their faces, I had the slow realization that none of them seemed to be truly happy people. You wouldn't know it looking at them—broad smiles, warm eyes, engaged conversations, laughter. But from what I knew of them privately, I didn't believe that any of them were truly happy or content. They all were talented, playful, yet restless spirits, constantly searching for approval through fame, and security through fortune and/or power. Most lived on a rollercoaster of emotions. There was very little self-awareness or genuine self-esteem in that room. And that included me. Later that night, I went to sleep with this heavy on my mind. The next morning, the doorbell rang, and Olga, the woman who cleaned my condominium every two weeks, was there with her usual smile. She started on the kitchen that was piled with dishes and wine glasses from the night before. A little later, I was working in my office on a screenplay, but my mind kept reviewing the previous night's insight. I wasn't happy. My friends weren't deeply happy either. For the first time in years, doubt crept into my mind that I may not be on the right path. Just then, I heard soft singing from the other room, and I glanced out the open door. There, in the kitchen, cleaning up after the "glamorous" party, was Olga. I watched her work, moving lightly and cheerfully as she tried to rescue my kitchen from the buried pots, dishes, and wine glasses, singing quietly to herself. I noticed that she had picked flowers from a tree outside and placed them in a vase on my coffee table. It was then that I realized that she was different in a very special way from my new society and me. I grasped then and there that Olga was the happiest person I was acquainted with. Olga, who left her son with her mother and drove in her late model car an hour through traffic from the poorer neighborhoods to the wealthier west side of Los Angeles to clean two houses a day. How did she find happiness with such (what I then considered) bleak circumstances? Her happiness was clearly not defined by her circumstances; she was living proof of that. And sadly, so were my friends and I. Happiness was not defined by our circumstances either. I understood that I had a big lesson to learn from Olga, and I am grateful for her exemplary teaching. I thought I knew what I wanted, but as it turned out, what I wanted was essentially a mirage. I was postponing happiness until I achieved certain goals—all of which were external circumstances that I believed would bring me happiness. But even when I began to achieve them, I still had emptiness inside.

As previously mentioned, I now personally define happiness as the daily experience of a meaningful life. For example, what makes my life meaningful is feeling that I am at one with what I perceive as the highest intelligent and compassionate force of the universe, which can be found within each of us. And I feel meaning when I am living authentically and am at one with my wife and my key relationships. And I experience meaning when I am doing my best work, which is in service to others and the world. And sometimes, I receive a quiet but overwhelming joy from nature. These aspects of life give me meaning and what I call happiness. Your definition of happiness is probably somewhat different from mine, but I believe that if you look deep enough, you will notice that your happiness is largely a result of having meaning in your life, and it is important to notice that meaning is not always accompanied by pleasure. For example, consider someone who works as a nurse in an emergency room. The circumstances there are by no means pleasurable much of the time, but many nurses will make a career of their work as they find that their lives become more meaningful. Why? Because they are living for something larger than themselves, they have gone beneath the surface of things and connected with their fellow humans beyond all social pretenses, and each and every day they know that they contribute to the well-being of someone who is suffering. To find meaning in the deepest currents of your life is a distinct kind of inner fulfillment that you will seek only at the point when you realize that pleasure alone is not ultimately fulfilling and that it is often followed by unhappiness. When you realize this, you have entered a new paradigm, and you will seek a new kind of life. Of course, to be happy, you do not need to reject pleasure, not at all, but to know the difference is crucial so that your choices support what is real and lasting and reject things that sap your life force.

WHY AREN'T WE HAPPY?

When we step back and examine our society, many of us may be quite surprised at how undereducated we are in terms of happiness. What we are taught is to be successful, with the unspoken message that success brings with it happiness—this is logical. But looking back at the statistics that the wealthiest societies in the world are medicating themselves for depression, anxiety, and sleep disorder, it is clearly not the case. Happiness is what every single person says he or she wants, but we know almost nothing about getting it. We are provided almost no education on how to obtain happiness, or even how to define it. I don't know about you, but when I was growing up, my friends and I received no guidance on how to become happy, no mentorship, no basic education. I cannot remember a single discussion at home, in school, or among my friends. It was not mentioned in our school curriculums, and there was no happiness textbook, class, conference, or afterschool discussion. In our community, parents held fundraising dinners to raise money for new equipment for the varsity football team, but there were no fundraisers for educating the youth on happiness.

Happiness is the most important universal intangible that every single person wants, yet it isn't on our radars as a topic to study, or even to discuss. It is as if it were to just spontaneously happen—like puberty. As teenagers, we all wanted happiness, but how to find it? The answer from the adults was no answer at all.

I'll give you a couple of examples of our ignorance when it comes to being taught the skills to become happier people. When I teach at conferences, I often ask for a show of hands. I say, "Raise your hand if when you were a teenager, you were taught a conflict resolution course in your high school." Usually, there is not one hand raised among hundreds of people. To me, this is astonishing because when we are teenagers, there is so much conflict in our lives, so much emotion, and for many, so much turmoil. And how are we taught to deal with conflict in relationships? We're not, we were constantly told *to behave*, but not *how* to behave—not how to resolve conflicts peacefully. The world is full of human conflict, and we are taught almost nothing about how to resolve it.

I also ask for a show of hands for all those who were taught breathing exercises in school to help manage emotions. This will cause some laughter and, again, rarely will anyone raise his or her hand. I then point out that, generally speaking, the only people in the United States who are taught how to breathe on a wide scale are pregnant women. Modern medicine seems to have acknowledged that breathing techniques help to manage fear and panic, to increase mental focus and clarity, and also to decrease physical pain, but apparently only for women giving birth. But what about the people in the burn unit? Or take a look in the orthopedic ward, where people are in traction with multiple broken bones. And what about our soldiers returning from war with posttraumatic stress disorder (PTSD)? They're not taught how to breathe to manage their physical and/or emotional pain. What about everyone else who is ever in pain or frightened or needs to focus amidst a chaotic situation? They're not taught how to breathe. Or a student taking an important test? No. Just pregnant women. It's incredible when you think about it.

Now you may be thinking: High school is really about learning things that help you get a job or prepare for college, and learning breathing techniques and conflict resolution classes won't help get you a job. This is perhaps true, but learning these skills may help you keep a job, or a marriage.

As I covered in my previous book, *A Life Worth Breathing*, I believe that daily medications for sleep, depression, and anxiety are highly appropriate for certain people with congenital dispositions or who are under extreme duress, and it is a blessing to be born at a time when such medications are available for those who need them, but I think it must be clear that one out of four women taking antidepressants and/or antianxiety drugs as an indefinite lifestyle, with the numbers climbing sharply, shows a trend toward the mass medication of society with no end in sight.

In my opinion, antianxiety drugs and antidepressants are like antihistamines; they give us the illusion of healing. They are essentially symptom suppressors, and symptom suppressors are not cures at all. To me, this is no less than a culture crisis, one that reaches for fast removal of symptoms rather than deeply affective solutions to root causes. This is indicative of our culture's current tendency for solving problems with a fast-food type solution. We don't have time to cook, so we eat fast food, but somehow we have time to engage in hours of social networking, TV, and video gaming.

Symptom suppressors delay or eliminate your impetus to explore why you can't sleep, or are depressed or anxious, and enable you to move on with your life without ever healing the root of the issue. You just take a pill, but it does not heal the cause, it only suppresses the symptom. We should welcome symptoms because symptoms are our warning lights. They are how our bodies communicate health challenges. To ignore and suppress them would be like being in your car and seeing a red warning light on your dashboard flashing, indicting low oil, and in response taking wire cutters and snipping the wire to the warning light. Now that pesky red flashing light is gone. Problem solved. (For those of you who are not knowledgeable about cars, the oil warning light will flash only when your car is perilously close to running out of oil, which will result in destroying your engine.) And so the cause remains, unhealed, beneath the surface. And using symptom suppressors can cause us to grow increasingly desensitized to our own body and emotions.

STARVING FOR INTIMACY

Not only is technology not making us happier but I believe it is also directly connected to our happiness spiraling downward. I visit over forty-five cities a year across the globe as a teacher, and speaker, leading seminars, workshops, and conferences. From this I am exposed to and work with a vast cross section of people in mostly large, industrial societies, and what I have observed is that an increasing number are dealing with issues of isolation and loneliness. We are starving for intimacy. I believe that one reason for this is that we are turning to technology for intimacy instead of turning to each other. We try to convince ourselves that three hundred virtual friends are better than five true friends. We are yearning for intimacy, yet as technology soars we find ourselves choosing to communicate through the *least* intimate form of communication available—text. Most children and teenagers do not use a Smartphone to talk at all; they send text messages—which is one step up from Morse code. We now have the ability to see and hear each other on the screen while we speak, but we'd rather communicate through text. (I think if someone came out with a Morse code app, it would sell.) To be clear, smartphones and social networking are fantastic tools but are, unfortunately, often used for misguided purposes.

This is not the first time major innovations have had antisocial ramifications. The first two crushing blows to the social bonds of the United States were the technological marvels of air conditioning and television. Not until after World War II did air conditioning enter the home of the average American. Before air conditioning, during hot summer weather, it was generally cooler out on the porch than it was inside the house. So people would often sit on their porches and chat with neighbors. The porch was, in essence, the householder's social connecting place to the neighborhood. Then the new invention called air conditioning began replacing porch sitting as people began staying indoors in the summer, where it was now much cooler. Domestic air conditioning now meant that the traditional deep porches were less frequently included in home design as they were no longer needed as a refuge from the heat. So air conditioning became a self-perpetuating necessity as homes were designed to include it and to exclude a deep front porch. The unintended social result was that people no longer went out to their porches in the evenings to meet with neighbors, and, almost without noticing, Americans began to live more isolated lives. It occurred almost without noticing because at about the same time, in the 1950s, the next technological marvel, television, entered the average air-conditioned American home. This created an even more exciting incentive not to venture outside and visit with neighbors— or for that matter, even speak with the people sitting right next to us, our own family members.

> **Television Statistics:** According to the A. C. Nielsen Co., the average American watches more than four hours of TV each day (or twenty-eight hours/week, or two months of nonstop TV-watching per year). In a sixty-five-year-long life, that person will have spent nine years staring at the television.

The Internet has had a similarly powerful socially disconnecting pull on people—away from *actual* interaction in exchange for massive *virtual* interaction. According to Wikipedia, "Overall Internet usage has seen tremendous growth. From 2000 to 2009, the number of Internet users globally rose from 394 million to 1.858 billion. By 2010, 22 percent of the world's population had access to computers with one billion Google searches every day, 300 million Internet users reading blogs, and two billion videos viewed daily on YouTube."

The popular rallying cry of this extraordinary innovation has been "we have never been so connected," but little attention had been given that to be "connected," you must stare at a flat screen and disconnect from the people who live with you or next door to you. One doctor I know, a married man with two teenage children, says, "In the evening, the four of us go to four different rooms and get online. We don't see each other much after dinner."

Put simply, when you are in communication with someone on the Internet (somewhere else), you are not interacting with the people in your home. Nor are you going out on the front porch to interact with your neighbors, or going to a meeting place to talk with people in real life and real time—to look into the eyes of a fellow human being and develop a more subtle and deeper relationship.

THE RISE OF THE FLAT SCREENERS AND THE DECLINE OF HAPPINESS

Mammals communicate with each other primarily without making sounds. Their survival depends upon their ability to read the body language of potential rivals and predators. A zebra knows the body language of the big cats, for example, and relies on this knowledge for its survival. It determines whether or not a lion will attack by immediate assessment of body language, not by words or even sounds.

According to studies, humans communicate ninety percent nonverbally.[11] When I first heard this statistic, I was stunned; I had no idea that language was so subordinate to nonverbal communication. But in the context of the linguistic development of humankind, it makes sense; proper language has, after all, only been in use about 100,000 years, whereas we communicated mainly nonverbally for some 2.3 million years prior. So, if we modern humans communicate ninety percent nonverbally, that means that whenever we communicate with text, we are using only ten percent of our communication potential. We are diluting communication

---

[11] Dr. Albert Mehrabian, author of *Silent Messages*, conducted several studies on nonverbal communication.

down to what I call the ten percent relationship . . . the very opposite of intimacy. Emotional intimacy involves personal knowledge of the deeper dimensions of another and is developed through trust, and trust can begin or end with a first glance because, like other mammals, we inherently know a great deal about each other through body language and other nonverbal cues. We often ascertain the trustworthiness of a person in mere seconds, without a word spoken. Based on nonverbal communication, we make life-altering decisions, especially as to whether or not to begin a relationship, whether or not you will accept a date with someone, or whether or not you will allow someone to look after your child. Many even decide whom to vote for in an election based on nonverbal cues that the candidates are projecting. This is how significant nonverbal communication is. We rely on it at the deepest level of our being. And what about our pets? A relationship between a human and an animal can be as deeply emotional as a relationship between humans. Of course we speak to our cat or dog a little, but the words are mostly inconsequential; the primary interaction between us is nonverbal. A relationship between a human and an animal is based on touch, presence, trust, loyalty, and especially a deep love. We can experience unspeakable joy with our pets and even great humor. And on the day that our beloved pet passes away, we can be as inconsolable as someone who has experienced the death of his or her own child.

What is ironic to me is that the scientists and inventors who are leading the way on this subject of what makes us human are the innovators of humanoid robots. In robotics, developers are making great strides in programing humanoid-type robots that have faces and can produce human expressions. Even more extraordinary is that robots are programmed to learn to make eye contact and to read and respond to human emotional expressions, tone of voice, and body language. They learn to see and respond to nonverbal cues. The designers also program human behavior into the robots as well, so that we will feel comfortable communicating with them. For example, I saw a demonstration of a humanoid robot where a scientist scolded it, raising her voice and saying "No" several times, as if she were scolding her dog. The robot read the scientist's face and tone and reacted accordingly. It lowered its eyes and head and appeared sad. The more the scolding went on, the more the robot appeared forlorn. Then the scientist praised the robot, and the robot again read the scientist's face and listened carefully to her tone of voice. The robot lifted its head, leaned forward, and smiled, encouraged and pleased by the praise.[12]

The strange irony is that we are teaching robots to make eye contact and watch for nonverbal cues because humans communicate ninety percent nonverbally, but meanwhile, we humans are now avoiding eye contact and nonverbal cues, opting instead to communicate through text and then adding smiley faces in order to humanize the message. We are humanizing the robot as we are voluntarily dehumanizing ourselves.

"But we are much more connected . . ."

If we are "much more connected," then why are we becoming less considerate? As I traveled the world over the past seven years, I noticed a fairly rapid decline in public behavior and manners. Increased focus on hand-held devices causes us to decrease our focus on our surroundings and on each other. As virtual social communication becomes commonplace, actual real-time social politeness and consideration seems to be deteriorating. With cell phones now commonplace, we seem to have forgotten that phone booths were partly created so everyone else didn't have to listen to us. People

---

[12] Kismet is a robot made at Massachusetts Institute of Technology by Dr. Cynthia Breazeal.

regularly speak on their cell phones in theaters and restaurants or while interacting with (or ignoring) service workers.

A woman in her early twenties told me that she feels that people of her generation are much less honest with each other as they communicate primarily through text and social media, and since the communication is not face to face, being dishonest is much easier.

We have all noticed that people absorbed with their hand-held devices are barely aware of what is going on around them. They run into others or stand in the way on sidewalks and other busy pedestrian areas as if stupefied. Collisions with poles or other objects are increasing, and physicians treat more and more people from these collisions that, while focusing on the virtual, slam into the actual world. A new report shows that in recent years, pedestrian injuries among sixteen- to nineteen-year-olds increased by twenty-five percent.

To suspect that the emotional collapse of the industrial world and the acceptance of massive use of pharmaceuticals to cope with life, rather than live it, are being at least partly linked to the technology explosion is not difficult. Our decline in happiness may be connected to our overly complex and ever-changing environment, which causes anxiety and confusion. A human continually confronted with massive change may withdraw into a more insular life in order to cope. Unfortunately, the commerce of the new technology overwhelmingly, though indirectly, supports this withdrawal by selling us solitary entertainment, such as video games and virtual, semi-controllable relationships through social media. So, it feeds on itself. We are becoming a population of what I call Flat Screeners, people who sit stationary in front of flat screens, engaging in imaginary worlds. Some are riveted to games, racking up meaningless points to claim an imaginary victory. When you watch someone passionately playing a video game, you witness a man completely absorbed in the virtual world, so much so that he sometimes becomes genuinely angry when he is losing. Even though he rationally knows that the game he is playing is only light and shadows and is not a true reality, he makes it into a temporary mental and emotional reality. Yet it amounts to no more than his dog chasing leaves blown by the wind. The activity is not wrong used simply as entertainment; it is benign. But when used as a constant escape from the actual world, it stifles growth and squanders your life span.

> *We have to choose our technology wisely. If we bring technology into our life, it should simplify our life. It should give us more free time, not take it away.*

An even more common phenomenon nowadays is our roaming through almost infinite information on the Internet, visiting websites for an average of, according to studies, a mere ten seconds, which tells us that our attention span has become alarmingly brief. Then there is social media or, as I call it, *the antisocial media*. As we peck away at small screens in the palm of our hand, we have the illusion of enormous connection with others when what is actually happening is we are physically isolating ourselves from each other. We avoid communication unless it is by text alone, the most impersonal means we have—as text is void of voice, vision, touch, and human presence. We are becoming like prisoners in solitary confinement, tapping on pipes in a desperate attempt to communicate with other prisoners somewhere in the gulag. But the difference is the prisoners have no choice but to communicate in this primitive way, whereas we have, by choice, exchanged true intimacy and friendship for the illusion of intimacy. And now we are strangely surprised that our souls are starving for connection and true purpose.

> *I text . . . therefore I am.*

Here are some notable statistics from the University of Gothenburg 2012 study of Facebook users:

Women spend on average eighty-one minutes per day on Facebook. • Men spend on average sixty-four minutes per day on Facebook. • The average user logs on to Facebook 6.1 times per day. • Seventy percent log in every time they start their computer or web reader. • Sixty-seven percent of young users use Facebook to kill time. • Women who use Facebook report feeling less happy and less content with their lives.

Perhaps we are inclined to the misapplication of social media because too many of us feel like we have little control over our actual reality. With virtual reality we have the sense of enormous, if not nearly absolute, power. This creates the illusion and feeling of control that accompanies the illusion of friendship and intimacy. But we must realize sooner or later that virtual reality is simply a newer word for mirage.

"Social Networking Leads as Top Online Activity Globally, Accounting for 1 in Every 5 Online Minutes" [13]

Every hour spent on the social media, especially with people you have never met in person, is an hour spent separated from those who love you and need you in physical proximity.

Social media is like the new white sugar of our time. The more we eat, the more we want and the worse we feel. People feel lonelier and lonelier and keep going back for more. Let me be clear that I do not believe that social media is evil. It is a wonderful way to communicate with loved ones who live far away, especially in

---

[13] It's a Social World: Social Networking Leads as Top Online Activity Globally, Accounting for 1 in Every 5 Online Minutes – from comScore 12/21/2011

very different time zones, or to post information to the family or a particular community of people, such as a church group, school, or organization. Social media helped to save lives during the Haiti earthquake crisis, as critical information, such as where to find food, medical treatment, and clean water, was posted and instantly available to hundreds of thousands. Social media has also been highly effective when used in political organizations, including the Arab Spring and the Green Revolution in Iran. There are hundreds more examples of excellent usage of social media. The damage from social media is not from its application; it is from its misapplication. It is truly an amazing tool when applied with wisdom.

And so we find ourselves again facing unintended consequences. It seems that the overuse of social media, text messaging, and gaming is causing our society, especially young people, to develop symptoms that remind me of Asperger syndrome—a mild autism. These symptoms include communication difficulties such as avoiding eye contact, inability to understand social rules and read body language, and difficulty in forming friendships. (I do not need to quote a scientific study that supports this; I know that if you have eyes to see, you have already seen this for yourself.)

Because of the inundation of flat screens in our lives, we are already having trouble deciphering the difference between life and entertainment. It is not likely that avatars in video games will enhance our real life and especially not our relationships. We do not need what are essentially puppets or dolls as friends, replacing real friends. What we need is to become self-aware before our computers do, both individually and as a society. If we do not, I believe that our happiness will continue to plummet, and we will continue to misuse technology at our own peril.

Electric communication will never be a substitute for the face of someone who with their soul encourages another person to be brave and true.

~ Charles Dickens

Recently, the newest version of *Call of Duty* video game reached $1 billion in sales in fifteen days.[14]

According to *A Media Studies Blog*, 65 percent of the US population is playing video games. The average gamer spends about eighteen hours a week playing video games. Eighteen- through forty-nine-year-olds make up the largest percentage of gamers at 49 percent.

[14] "New 'Call of Duty' fastest game in history to reach $1 billion." By Ben Fritz *Los Angeles Times* December 05, 2012.

THE AGE OF WISDOM

We know that the world is in a period of rapid change and unpredictability, but what remains constant, actual, and vital is our connection to each other and our source. The answers to these questionable times can be elusive, but the answer to healing and revitalizing yourself is crystal clear: by accelerating your own personal transformation. I believe we must move from the Information Age to the Age of Wisdom. Information isn't enough; without wisdom, information is just data. Many of our problems today are created by very intelligent and educated people, so until *we* change, the same problems will repeat themselves—the same conflicts, the same type of issues, just a different era. We must now heal and empower ourselves so that we are worthy of our New Cambrian world.

You know, my friends, we can refuse to live our lives in virtual reality. We can say aloud that we want the real thing and we want to make a difference in that reality. We know that we do not need virtual friends; we need real friends. We can choose not to pretend that Facebook is as rich as face-to-face time with true friends. How many times have we seen children in a park trying to get their mother (or father) to play with them while she (or he) chats on a smartphone or exchanges text messages? The essential question ends up not being about science but about what makes us human, what we ultimately want, and how to acquire it. And, sometimes, what needs to be discarded from our life entirely.

In the next section of this book, I am going to introduce you to a course of action, the three imperatives, that you can implement to accelerate change from the inside out. I call them imperatives because I don't really think we can change the world without changing ourselves. You have an internal technology within you now, along with all of the apps you need in your heart, mind, and body to elicit a personal renaissance, but you need to upload this knowledge and begin to use it. This is a direct program to empower you to access the inner knowledge and the power you possess but which lies dormant. And you can begin today.

PART TWO:
THE TECHNOLOGY OF HAPPINESS

We have forgotten that we are meant to be more like lighthouses, luminous and sharing our light with the world, but we have encased our bright lamp within a metal cage and then covered it with concrete. Once darkened, we feel lonely and isolated, and so we compensate by hanging what amounts to tinsel and Christmas lights around the tower. In other words, we cut ourselves off from each other, encasing our emotions in scar tissue from past traumas and heartbreak, diminishing our natural power and inner beauty. In our self-made isolation, we then overcompensate by taking desperate measures to grasp at some semblance of intimacy. The tinsel and Christmas lights take many forms, such as social power, enhanced sexual beauty, material wealth, and so on, but it is all nothing compared to the inner light that we already posses but have hidden from the world and sometimes even from ourselves.

The capacity for meaningful transformation or even a complete renaissance is present in each of us; we simply need to activate the innate internal technology that we already have, and have had, by learning some simple yet powerful skills that are currently not being taught on a wide scale. This work is for people from all walks of life and levels of fitness, whether or not they have a stiff body or a rigid schedule. It is my mission to help people remember who they are and what they are capable of, and to provide tools for them to empower themselves and live a more meaningful life. I have distilled the technology of happiness into three primary disciplines. The reason this knowledge is not being taught on a wide scale is not because of a global conspiracy, but because, from a monetary point of view, it is not profitable to empower people to find happiness within, and what is not profitable is not advertised, and what is not advertised ceases to exist on our flat screens. No advertiser is going to tell you that his or her product will not contribute to your happiness whatsoever and that you would be far better to ignore this product and instead switch off your television and spend more time with your family. Quite the opposite, a marketing campaign exists to convince you that if you purchase a particular product, even if it is dish soap, your happiness will be enhanced.

Positive, self-motivated evolution is perhaps one of the most important endeavors worth spending our most precious resource—our time—on, as it may ultimately be our only road to happiness and a meaningful life.

The first imperative: We need to become self-aware.

The second imperative: Live as if your time and your life span were the same thing.

The third imperative: Learn a daily regime that heals and empowers you, and practice it one hour a day.

IMPERATIVE 1:
WE NEED TO BECOME SELF-AWARE

The Imperative of Self-Study

I saw the headline of a magazine article that read, "Could the Net become self-aware?" A more relevant question for us is, "Can we humans become self-aware?" That is the question of our time. As I pointed out in the beginning of this book, many of the preeminent experts in artificial intelligence believe that a computer will become self-aware and its intelligence will exceed that of our most brilliant human beings and that by around 2030 some experts believe its intelligence will be so great that, comparatively, we humans will be like insects. If their predictions are true, then it will be humankind's greatest irony that we create a machine that becomes self-aware before we do, not to mention more intelligent. I will leave the predictions of both the benefits and the unintended consequences of this outcome to the futurists who are currently spending night and day exploring the many possibilities of this potential scenario. But whether this occurs or does not occur exactly this way, we humans must seriously consider no longer distracting ourselves as a way of life and, instead, focus on the most exciting and empowering prospect of all—a meaningful life and a deeper level of happiness that will also have a healing impact on society and the planet. One of the most beautiful life principles is that when you develop a meaningful life, you add more meaning to the lives of others. When you heal yourself, you help to heal your family. For example, every book that you have ever read that has touched your spirit was written by someone who achieved a deeper level of meaning in his or her life, which inspired the creation of the book, and in that way a torch of knowledge and inspiration is passed from hand to hand, or better said, from heart to heart.

WHAT IS SELF-AWARENESS?

Put simply, while awareness is our ability to sense and observe the exterior world and our physical bodies, in the context of this book, self-awareness is our ability to observe our interior world, including our motives, character, and behavior. It is commonly accepted that human beings are self-aware creatures. I believe this is true, but only up to a point. The evidence of human history and even the most basic observation of our family members and our own behavior reveal that human beings have only fragmented behavioral and motivational self-awareness.

For example, you probably know someone who thinks he's funny, and he is sometimes, but most people just find him annoying. People have tried to tell him, but he doesn't listen. He's still convinced he's funny. Or you know someone who believes that he is respected in his business, but in fact, he is feared and not respected at all. He doesn't seem to know the difference. And it is likely that you know someone who believes that her weight gain is because of her metabolism. She doesn't seem to understand that her weight gain is because of her excessive overeating habits. Everyone knows but her.

These are everyday examples of people holding false beliefs about themselves. The society around them is aware of aspects of their personality and behavior that they themselves are not. We all have varying degrees of fragmentary self-awareness. When it comes to ourselves, we all have a blind side. This fragmentary self-awareness is one of the central causes of unhappiness, because most of us do not know what drives us to behave in the way we do or make the choices we make. In fact, many of the most renowned philosophers and sages through time believed or believe that it is *the central cause* of unhappiness. We don't need the Internet or our laptop to become self-aware; we can predict right now what a self-aware, hyperintelligent computer would say to us after carefully examining human history and the daily news. It would say, "What humanity needs at the macro level and individual level is to become self-aware. Until you achieve this, history will repeat itself, corruption and crime will continue, personal suffering will continue."

Perhaps it is time to apply Silicon Valley-style research and innovation *to ourselves*.

REVEALING YOUR BLIND SIDE

The first step to becoming self-aware is through self-study. A common term for self-study is self-reflection, implying that we are looking at an inner mirror, so to speak, and seeing ourselves in the mirror, we make adjustments. In this way, we become our own mentors on the path of life. To quote Lao Tzu, the renowned Taoist philosopher, "At the center of your being you have the answer; you know who you are and you know what you want." This is the goal of self-study.

Some of us excel due to our parents' influence. Some of us excel in spite of our parents' influence. But for most of us, it is a combination of both: We excel partly due to our parents and also by working against the negative habits or thought patterns they ingrained in us.

The study of your own personality and inherent tendencies is crucial for finding and transforming thought patterns that I call our inner terrorist. Our inner terrorist is the part of us that tends to sabotage our best intentions, our relationships, and our career—anything that we allow it to have its way with. In some cases, this phenomenon is caused from fear of failure; in other cases it is caused by fear of success. Either way, the inner terrorist must be recognized for what it is, and we must work to tame this demon. In some people, it is the inner terrorist that drives them to worldly success, because the voice of their terrorist fiercely pushes them to excel by dominating others. In this case, the inner terrorist torments other people too. This is one of the most difficult syndromes to change, because if a person has achieved great power, prestige, or wealth by being selfish, cruel, and ruthless, then healing the inner terrorist threatens that person's position in life. For a person in this situation to ardently want to change would most likely require either a monumental epiphany from something like a near-death event or a great tragedy to motivate them to seek a new way of being.

Through self-study, you can become acquainted with your habits, strengths, and weaknesses until you can plainly see, understand, and alter them. If you do not, your inner terrorist will stay right with you for the rest of your days.

Most people confuse happiness with pleasure gained from outside sources—pleasure triggers such as food, sex, cigarettes, alcohol, and various drugs, both legal and illegal. Other external triggers for pleasure are material wealth, power over others, and for some, fame. And now it is increasingly common to seek pleasure through distraction dispensed right in the palm of your hand, no matter where you are in the world. Notice that in all of the examples, the causes for pleasure come from external circumstances, and in the case of electronic media, from the illusion of experiencing a parallel reality.

So many of the actions we take are intended to distract us from negative circumstances rather than changing them. Here is an example of a man, I'll call him Doug, who is fundamentally unhappy yet has never studied himself to discover the reasons why he is unhappy.

Doug, thirty years old, hates his day job and is bored with his life, so at meals he chooses foods that will cause his body to trigger a large amount of dopamine by ingesting excessive amounts of fats, sugar, and salt (fast food), smoking cigarettes, imbibing alcohol, etc. This makes him feel better for a little while, but over time he becomes addicted to the fats, sugar, salt, cigarettes, and alcohol and so increases the dosage or frequency of the dosage. During his workday, he also consumes various energy drinks and 16 oz. sodas to "keep him going." From the high dosages of salt, sugar, and caffeine from these drinks, Doug's blood pressure soars, and he sometimes gets jittery and anxious. In the evening his body crashes, exhausted from work, his extreme diet, frustration, and boredom, and so he chooses his next course of action: He plays video games in which he will likely save the universe for four or more hours while he imbibes at least a few beers and possibly smokes some cannabis. Finally, he takes his nightly dose of sleep aids and climbs into his bed, bathed in the blue light of the chattering TV, and struggles to fall asleep.

What is missing from these unexplored lifestyle choices is that as long as Doug follows this course, his life circumstance will not improve, but will only worsen over time. Doug expresses to his friends his wish for change and complains about his life on a daily basis but does nothing to change his behavior or his situation. This is because he has not even begun the journey of self-discovery. He is unaware that his life situation was created by himself and could be changed by himself. On the contrary, Doug sees his situation as unchangeable. To add more salt to the wound, Doug regularly purchases lottery tickets as his single and last hope for escaping his life of suffering for a better one, which of course he does not win, and that makes him feel even more foolish. So, Doug falls into depression and eventually goes to his doctor for his high blood pressure medication refill and to discuss "if antidepressants are right for him."

What is Doug feeling? He feels frustrated and confined by a life that by his own standards has no meaning. He knows he is capable of much more but does not know what to do. He feels anger about his circumstances and is privately ashamed of his helplessness. But because he feels hopeless, believing he can do nothing to change his circumstances, he makes multiple choices to suppress his negative feelings. For example, when he feels shame, rather than make a plan to change his circumstances, he eats or drinks, or he smokes something that gives him a wonderful feeling, covering over his feeling of shame. And he learns to do this each time he feels a negative emotion (symptom) rather than taking time each evening to understand what he needs to change in himself in order to change his experience of life.

Self-study leads to self-awareness, and self-awareness empowers us to truly transform and stop repeating the same negative choices that undermine our life. It solves apex problems, and solving apex problems creates a domino effect of positive change.

Sometimes for our life to take flight it is critical to change our occupation or career, but sometimes even changing our occupation would not make any difference, because our profession is not the cause of our unhappiness, and if we chose to change our profession, our unhappiness would follow us. Our chosen profession can be empty or full regardless of its stature in society. Mahatma Gandhi was a lawyer and arose to became renowned, not for his profession but for his method of conflict resolution, inspiring worldview, and way of life.

One of the most powerful spiritual leaders among women in the history of the United States is Anne Hutchinson (1591–1643). She was married to a farmer and was a practicing midwife. She also had thirteen children of her own. Not glamorous or wealthy, she was well known for her kindness and healing capacity, and people gathered from all around to hear her speak of life, healing, and spirituality.

One of the things these people had in common was that they had ordinary professions but were not defined or confined by them;

they were self-aware, rose beyond their occupations, and became beacons that helped other people to find deeper meaning in their own lives.

Self-study cannot be underestimated. Knowledge is more powerful than belief. Belief in a higher ideal alone isn't usually enough for most people to find meaning and happiness in their lives. How many people have you met who are 100 percent invested in a belief paradigm yet are emotionally hanging on by a thread, or who often behave badly? And how many people have you met who adhere fervently to a religion yet also lie in bed awake at night with insomnia or grind their teeth in their sleep or need antidepressants to cope with a life they cannot reconcile? (It isn't only atheists who are taking antianxiety or antidepressant medications.) This is where the work part of spiritually comes in. We have in our hearts what we believe to be true, and we follow our faith or the religion that our families followed, but we cannot seem to integrate what we believe with how we live and how we feel emotionally day to day. Self-awareness doesn't change your religion; it helps you to integrate it into your life. Self-awareness doesn't ask you to adopt a religion; it offers you a clearer picture of what you want and who you are.

It is significant to note that from Jesus to Buddha, to Lao Tse and Mohamed, and countless other renowned teachers of the ages (as well as many recent scientific studies) put forth many of the same essential philosophies of life. One is that happiness is not determined by your external circumstances. Each one taught that (I'm using modern metaphors) you have access to an internal technology that is available at any time, but you must choose to switch it on. Socrates is credited for the simple yet pinnacle ethos, "Know thyself." Self-awareness through self-study is a prerequisite teaching of nearly all of the master teachers. There are many methods of self-study, from working with a skilled therapist to contemplative meditation; there are many highly useful techniques. But one of the most rapid methods to reveal your blind side is by asking yourself high-level, illuminating questions, studying your own answers, and then, empowered by your new knowledge, taking action.

THE BOOK OF YOUR LIFE

What is a high-level question? A high-level question is one that generates high-level thinking, which will then engender a high-level answer. This is a technique successfully utilized by teachers through the ages, from Zen Buddhist and Sufi teachers to Anthony Robbins, yet is sadly one of the most underutilized transformational techniques. I am now going to lead you through a series of questions, and I want you to answer them in a particular way. For this to work, you must follow my directions exactly. What you will have in your hands at the end of the exercise is what I call "the book of your life."

What you will need:

1. Writing materials. It is preferable for you to use pen and paper, but if you need to, use a computer keyboard. Make sure the pen has dark ink and moves smoothly across the paper. Use good quality paper.
2. A quiet and solitary place.
3. One hour of time.
4. A timer that will beep.

5. Absolutely no interruptions. That means all smartphone's will be off and not on vibrate. No children or pets to distract you. This hour is yours.

When you are prepared and ready, you will answer these ten questions in the time frame that you are directed to, five minutes each. It would be possible to get lost in pondering these questions for weeks. But instead of engaging only the analytical part of your brain, you will be using many parts of your mind and even stored memory from your body. So, stay within the constructed time frame.

You will set your timer to five minutes. Read the question and then press the start button on the timer. Then proceed to writing down the answer on the paper. When the timer goes off, stop. Go to the next question, and so on. What you write here will have as much power as the truth you give the answers. Be completely honest with yourself as you answer these questions, more honest than you have ever been in your life up to now. The answers to these central questions will not be found on Google. Answer in this way, and I guarantee that you will be rewarded with a new way of seeing your life.

Set your time to five minutes now.

The Book of Your Life

Part I

Question #1:

How do you define happiness? Have you thought about it recently? Because what makes you happy when you're twenty is very different from what makes you happy when you're forty. It changes every decade. How do you expect to find happiness if you aren't even sure what it is? To become truly happy, you must have a clear definition of what truly brings you joy and fulfillment. Write down how you define happiness now.

Question #2:

Who is the most joyful adult that you know? You do not have to know him or her well, but he or she needs to be a living person you are acquainted with. It could be your mother or a barista who makes coffee for you. It can be anyone. (Don't list a child; the person must be an adult.) Identify who the most joyful adult you know is, and write down a few ways in which he or she expresses joy.

Question #3:

What was the happiest period of time in your life thus far? And what made it so? It may have been a time many years ago; it may be the period that you are in now. Identify the happiest period of time in your life so far and write down some details of why it was so happy.

Question #4:

Who are your true friends? (And I don't mean Facebook friends.) Who could you call at three in the morning to ask for help in an emergency, and that friend would not hesitate to help you? For whom would you get out of bed at three in the morning if he or she called and needed your help? We spend a lot of time thinking about whom we want to go to bed with; maybe we should think a little more about whom we would get out of bed for. Our truest friends are those with whom we share our most precious moments as well as comfort in our darkest hours. List your true friends by name.

Question #5:

If you had to flee the country and could bring only one medium-sized suitcase and had thirty minutes to pack, what would you bring? You will not have to pack for your children, as they each get their own suitcase. You will not have to stuff your pet into the suitcase; you can bring your pets along. No, you cannot stuff cash into the case; where you are going, your cash and credit cards are no good. You will arrive penniless with the exception of the things in this suitcase. This is not to identify survival equipment; imagine you will have all the basics you need. This is to identify your most valuable possessions—the things most precious to you, such as treasured letters, photographs, heirlooms, sentimental objects, etc.

Question #6:

What is your code of ethics? Notice that we have two sets of ethics: One set we practice when calm and happy; and another when we feel afraid or someone has offended us. The work is to have one set of ethics. Take five minutes to write these down as bullet points and try to limit this list to ten ethics or less. Do not oversimplify by writing down one-word answers. For example, if you were to write *honesty* as one of your ethics, then follow it up with a few specifics as to what you mean by that. Err on the side of too much versus too little. I encourage you to not write down what you were taught as a child, but what you believe now, based on your life experience.

Question #7:

If you knew that you would be deceased fifteen minutes from now, what would you regret not having done or said in your life? Do not write down actions that you regret; be clear, the question is about *what you regret <u>not</u> having done or said*. For example, "I wish I had told him that I love him . . ."

Question #8:

What do you need to do to improve your communication skills so you have less conflict and more understanding in your relationships? Every single one of us has some communication handicaps. Perhaps you speak indirectly. Perhaps you expect others to know what your needs are without your asking for them. What are your weak links in your communication, and what do you need to do to improve your communication skills so you have less conflict and more understanding in your relationships?

Question #9:

What is your mission in this life? Not necessarily your profession, but what you are on this earth to do? The big picture. Some of us are fortunate that our mission and our profession are the same. For example, my mother was a high school history teacher but was frequently voted most popular teacher of the year because she was known to help raise the self-esteem of her students. So, I would say that her mission was to help raise the self-esteem of her students while she happened to teach them history. Teaching history was her vocation, but not her mission. Some of us have yet to discover our mission in this life; if this applies to you and you have no idea how to answer this question, then think of what the people who you respect have told you. What have they pointed out to you about yourself that you have ignored? Some people have a lot of money and power but are still playing it small because they haven't done what they know needs to be done for the good of all, and they know they could do it. What is your mission in this life?

Question #10:

How do you sabotage yourself from fulfilling your life's mission? Explain the ways that your inner terrorist sabotages your life's mission. List some of its tactics that you have witnessed again and again.

You can now put your paper away for a day or so and come back to it later for part II of the exercise, or continue on now if you wish and have the time.

Part II

Now let's go over what you have revealed. I will add commentary for you to consider and also some homework.

1. **How do you define happiness?** You have defined what happiness is for you. Read and reread this definition. Keep this definition in plain sight—on your wall or in your wallet or handbag. Keep it in the forefront of your mind and, throughout the course of your days, determine if your actions support or deter your happiness. Also, share what makes you happy with your family and significant other. At the beginning of each day, read this definition aloud to yourself. Over time, the definition will evolve; this is natural, so feel free to amend it as time moves on. You have made the first important step toward happiness by processing this simple yet powerful question. Each step on your journey of self-awareness will move more quickly hereafter.

2. **Who is the most joyful adult that you know?** You have identified the most joyful person you know. Isn't it interesting who this is in your life? Isn't it equally fascinating whom you did not choose? Study his or her actions and attitudes, learn from this person. If it is possible, ask to interview him or her and discover how they look at the world. If you feel reluctant to do this, if this feels silly, think carefully about how it feels "normal" to seek advice for almost anything other than happiness.

3. **What was the happiest period of time in your life thus far?** You have identified the happiest period of time in your life. What made this period of time so amazing? It may be that you were in love, it may be a time when you had a

strong community around you, and it may be a time when your children were still small. Whatever the cause, notice if your happiness in this period had much to do with money. Was this period of time so happy because you had a lot of money? This exercise will help you to see what truly has lasting and profound impact on you and what doesn't, and to what degree money impacts your happiness.

4. **Who are your true friends?** You have identified your true friends. Your homework is to tell them, one at a time. It is so important that you learn to express love. Send each friend a handwritten card and tell him or her how you feel. Not a text message, not an email, not a voicemail, but a hand-written card. This might be the best card he or she receives all year. (If that person ever has to flee the country and can bring only one medium-sized suitcase, this card will likely be in it.) Tell these people that you did this exercise where you were asked who are your truest friends and that they are on this list, and you thought that they would want to know. Consider how to invest more time and loving care with these treasured friends and less time with virtual friends. Let us learn to hold our friends close to us and not wait for the good-byes to express how much we care.

5. **If you had to flee the country and could bring only one medium-sized suitcase and had thirty minutes to pack, what would you bring?** You have identified your most precious possessions. The possessions that matter the most. It is amazing to see what made it into this hypothetical suit-case—and, just as illuminating, what didn't make it in. This exercise is to help you put your possessions, all of them, into perspective. We typically invest vast sums of money

and even go into debt to acquire things that ultimately mean very little to us. Your homework is first to have a yard sale to eliminate the clutter of near useless objects that you have accumulated, and secondly, when you find yourself in a store lusting after an item for sale, ponder for a moment if this would even have a chance of being selected to be included in that special suitcase.

6. **What is your code of ethics?** You determined your code of ethics. Notice that we discuss ethics every day in the form of complaining of other people's behavior around the subjects of driving, money, politics, and especially romantic relationships. But we often do not look at our own actions and impact on others. With a tone of friendship, share your code with your family. Create a dialogue around ethics and ask to know the ethics of those closest to you. Not in a challenging way, this is not meant to be a forum for debate. Instead, ask about ethics with the understanding that it is intimate knowledge, so be especially polite and sensitive when discussing them—including ethics with which you disagree. Challenge your own code so that you go to a deeper level. Explore ethics together, such as, if you believe in nonviolence, do you hold to it under any and all circumstances? Most people don't; their ethic of nonviolence is conditional, and this is absolutely normal. What is important is that you become clear about the conditions and nuances of your ethics to become even more knowledgeable of yourself.

7. **If you knew that you would be deceased fifteen minutes from now, what would you regret not having done in your life?** You have listed your regrets. This is a most

surprising list for some of us. As I have mentioned before, people near death are not focused on what they have done but on what they did not do, on opportunities for happiness and fulfillment that were squandered. These are things that truly haunt us as we face the end of our mortal life. So, this list of regrets based on a hypothetical imminent death is to become your high-priority to-do list. Because it is unlikely that you will be dead in fifteen minutes, you still potentially have an opportunity to change the course of your life. Look carefully at your list; some opportunities have come and gone forever, but many are still possible. This list of missed opportunities is a way of reverse-engineering your priorities. It identifies the most important actions you can take to bring more happiness and meaning into your life. Waste no time—make certain that the things on this list are crossed off as you fulfill each of them. Let us all leave this world with as few regrets as humanly possible.

8. **What do you need to do to improve your communication skills so you have less conflict and more understanding in your relationships?** You have determined which communication skills you need to develop and improve. This is also a to-do list. To enhance your communication skills is very significant as it immediately improves your relationships. In private, record yourself speaking aloud about your feelings. See page 75.

9. **What is your mission in this life?** You have identified your mission in this life. Your work now is to make certain that your choices and actions support your mission. Like your definition of happiness, post your mission in plain sight or in your wallet or handbag. Spend more time with friends

and associates who see you in this way and will be supportive; this will help raise your self-esteem and confidence in your mission.

10. **How do you sabotage yourself from fulfilling your life's mission?** You have identified one of the most insidious achievements of your inner terrorist. In my workshops where I present these ten questions, I carefully observe the participants writing down their answers, and this is the answer that people have the least hesitation to write. They need no time to ruminate about it because most of us know exactly how we sabotage ourselves, how our inner terrorist prevents us from shining bright in this world. Your work now is to do everything in your power to support your mission and to make certain that you spend time with those who see you in this way and do not cause you to doubt your path.

You have just written the book of your current life, a concise, direct, and powerful overview of critical knowledge that will help bring your life into focus and articulate what is of true value to you and what needs to be set aside. This will help accelerate your journey to the daily experience of meaning and happiness. Why is this simple exercise so powerful? It is most likely because you received almost no mentorship regarding happiness, and you have never been asked to answer these questions before—certainly not all of them, one after the other in a single sitting. The answers to the ten questions paint a picture, a concise image of your life at the present moment, but you may also have noticed that there is a cumulative effect from the entire one-hour program; you may feel an accruing emotional opening. I recommend that you take notes to record any insights that may percolate to the surface as a result of this work.

Take the heart of this exercise into your daily life. When presented with a difficult situation, tune into yourself and ask yourself high-level questions to help you determine your response. This is a way of retraining the mind to automatically select high-level questions to solve challenging areas of your life.

Here are some more examples of high-level questions to ask yourself during challenging times:

- Is there another way I can look at this situation that would improve the relationship/s of the person/people involved in the process of fixing the problem? If the relationship is more important than the disagreement (and it usually is), how can I reinforce the relationship and yet stick to my principles?
- Have I lost my gratitude?
- Is there a way I can accomplish this task and make it more enjoyable?
- If someone came to me for advice on this same type of problem, what would I advise him or her to do?

UTILIZING TECHNOLOGY TO INCREASE SELF-AWARENESS

It is arguable that when it comes to personal media and electronic devices, we use technology in every way except in the ways that could actually help us to become more self-aware.

We love to record ourselves at our best—at weddings, athletic events, parties, and celebrations—but when it comes to recording ourselves when we are upset, we shun the idea. We do not want to hear or see ourselves when we are angry, petty, afraid, or in grief. We have a habit of pretending these expressions never happened. Like the way we sort through snapshots of ourselves, keeping the flattering photos and throwing away the less than flattering ones. We have conditioned ourselves to seeing only images and videos in the way we want to see ourselves, but not as an honest portrayal or account of our entire personality and behavior.

Consider utilizing home technology for self-observation and reflection. Begin with audio recordings. Virtually every cell phone and smartphone now has an audio recording device that comes as a built-in feature, so if you own a cell phone of some kind, you already have this tool.

Your exercise is to record yourself speaking candidly about your feelings regarding a difficulty you're having with a friend or family member. In three days or so listen carefully to the recording in private. (It is likely that you will be very surprised how you sound, especially if you have never heard yourself played back from a recording device. Don't let that scare you off; stay focused and listen to the content.) Listen to your choice of words and tone of voice. This is an amazing tool for self-reflection. The audio recording doesn't lie or exaggerate or take any bias; it is purely objective. By studying yourself in this way, you will begin to understand more clearly how others hear you when you speak about your feelings. And it is likely that you will decide to change your choice of words and to even present your feelings in a new way when the time comes to actually address your feelings with someone directly.

After doing this exercise a few times, find a willing partner to record a conversation with. Don't choose someone with whom you are angry. Record a conversation about something that is emotional for you but not upsetting to the other person or confrontational, yet still very personal. Then, again, wait a few days before listening to the recording. When you do listen, you will learn even more about how you communicate in a conversation.

If you and your significant other are brave, consider recording a conversation about a subject that you do not see eye to eye on. (Not contentious.) Record the conversation, and then listen to it in a few days. You can listen back separately or sitting together. I suggest that you take notes and then discuss the notes later. Doing this on video would be even better, but save that until later after you are acclimated to witnessing yourself through visual media. The recordings can in a way act as a third person, an impartial witness.

This method of using technology for self-reflection has many benefits; it may also help you to clean up any negative speaking habits as well.

It's not personal; it's just business . . .

Self-awareness is not complete if you do not bring this practice into your business life as well as your personal life. We should not have one set of rules of behavior for home and one for business. There is no difference. There really isn't. Perhaps you have heard the term "Sunday Christian." That is a derisive term used to refer to someone who attends Christian church services on Sundays while not adhering to the doctrines of the religion the other six days of the week. Whatever your creed or religion, make certain that you reflect it in your career or business. Study how you speak to people at work. Try to notice how differently you speak to those in positions above you compared to those who work for you. To work as a subordinate to a supervisor who is a poor communicator is extremely frustrating, as it will negatively impact your work by misunderstanding what you were asked to do. It wastes everyone's time. Crystal clear communication makes everything more efficient and generates more team cohesion. As a rule, we tend to be more careful of how we say things when dealing with supervisors or employers because there are potential consequences, whereas in dealing with subordinates we mistakenly believe that the reverse is often true. Sometimes foremen or assistant managers can make their subordinates' work life a living hell with constant verbal abusive and caustic language.

Strive to become a leader who incorporates decency and respect into all communications, and you will find that you are not less effective but more.

Our communication with others during business hours is really the main forum for our practice and one with which we create our reputation. The more we study ourselves, thereby becoming self-aware, the more effective we will be in our work and the more well-regarded we will become. You will excel at business and also at your personal relationships. Recording meetings with colleagues, associates, and subordinates can be extremely helpful in your self-study. I record my lectures and seminars at least once a month. Later, I listen back and critique my work. I am never 100 percent satisfied. I always hear many things I would like to have said differently or with a different tone. I cannot stress enough how important this is and that there is always room to improve.

THE DISCOVERY OF SYMPTOMATIC BEHAVIOR

Once you begin working with the three imperatives, you'll notice that one component will reinforce the others. For example, as you begin to practice breath-initiated movement, that work will help you with self-awareness. One of the most radical discoveries you will have at some point is that much of your behavior is symptomatic. A symptom is an indication of something, which means that some of your choices and some of the ways that you react to others are not actually part of your personality as you have always presumed. For example, if you have suppressed a great deal of grief, it takes a lot of energy to keep your grief buried inside your body unexpressed. This will cause your system to be disharmonious, and that will cause you to behave in certain unsociable ways. But when you one day release your buried grief, purging the past so to speak, you may find that a certain behavior has disappeared because that behavior was only a symptom of your suppressed grief. You might also discover that once you release suppressed negative emotions, you will begin to feel happy.

As one student so aptly stated:

For years I pursued spiritual knowledge through medita-
tion and reading spiritual books. A lot of my questions were
answered, and my mind was released from the confusion and
conflict that I had about life. But in my day-to-day life my
personal relationships were less than ideal, and I was still not
happy, not really. When I discovered yoga, and in particular
the breathing, the pain in my body was gradually removed,
and with it went the pain from my past. When this happened,
joy and contentment poured in. It seems that, for me, happiness
came through the desire and discipline of letting go of my past
and reconciling to it.

The above statement could have been said by any one of thousands of people. I hear variations of this kind of epiphany every
week as people share their insights from their yoga practice or special breathing sessions.

For me, it was no different; once I was out of pain, I became,
over time, more interested in helping others heal and transform,
and this gave my daily life great meaning. But also I learned that
to maintain happiness demands some degree of conscious work in
keeping my heart open and not rearmoring myself.

This is a key principle of healing, to understand that we store
emotions from our past in our own bodies. It is as if our heart-
breaks, trauma, and shame are the bars and bolts of a prison cell.
Imprisoned, we wait for someone to come into our lives with a key
to open the door. Song after song has been written of this long-
ing. So many of us wait for a prince or maiden to come and rescue
us from our self-built dungeon. We wait and wait, locked away in
solitary confinement. Our friends visit us at the barred door of the
prison and give us some comfort, advice, and camaraderie, but they
cannot release us from this self-imposed cell. The key to the door

is possessed by only one person: the key is in our own hand. We are told this again and again throughout our lives, but we do not believe it. We possess the key, but the problem is we do not know how to use it, and we aren't even aware that the key is a key. This is why self-study is absolutely critical in enabling us to understand what tools are available, what needs to be repaired, and what needs to be healed. But all of this work cannot be done with your mind alone. The third imperative must be included for holistic healing. Reconciling to the past will free you to build a new future and to truly release old damaging relationships. This will open the door, finally, to new healthy relationships, but the door must be opened by releasing it, not by kicking it down.

KNOCKING ON THE TEMPLE DOOR

If you wish to enter a temple with a locked door, one way of doing this would be by taking a battering ram and bashing the door in. This would get you in, but it would destroy the door, and you would never be invited back. A more polite and considerate method would be to respectfully knock on the door and wait to be invited in. You continue knocking patiently until the door is opened from the inside. The knocking is your breath, your inhaling and exhaling; the door is the entryway to your internal life and power. Force is not always the best tool for healing. Sometimes it is, but you must know the difference and when to use it. Because so many of us feel disempowered, we constantly look for opportunities to gain more power of any kind. But gaining more power is not always the answer. When we feel stuck, we naturally feel the urge to acquire more power, like putting a larger engine in a car that is stuck in the mud. But if the car is chained to a stonewall, you can keep adding more and more power and not move a single inch forward.

Advertisers seem to have noticed our sense of disempowerment and have answered us with more and more products and services with the adjective "power" added to the title. Power clothing, power bars, power everything. And now other similar adjectives are being thrown at us: *magnum, ultra, max.* These words wouldn't be seen on thousands of products if we as a society felt powerful. It is because of our sense of powerlessness that we want to buy things that might give us even a bit more power. But sometimes to move forward, you simply need to unchain yourself from the past. Then you may find that you have all the power that you need once the past has been released. To let go of the past may be the most meaningful action you will ever take. To do so requires a process of healing and often forgiveness, and this process can't be skipped over in your quest to transform yourself. This is yet another reason why self-awareness is so critical, because without it we may remain chained and imprisoned to our past for our entire lifetime. I have met many people in their later years still waiting for someone to open the door to their cells.

YOGA AND MEN

It is my experience that women have more of a proclivity toward healing, spirituality, and yoga due to their more nurturing and emotionally aware nature. Women are permitted by society to express their feelings, to cry, and to be sensitive. Women often learn to dance at a very early age, so they learn to perceive their bodies as a vehicle for beauty, grace, and expression. In these dance classes they learn coordination and to stretch slowly and move with awareness. Women have a natural disposition to sharing their bodies. First with a lover and then while pregnant with a child. After giving birth, a woman's body continues to be the source of the infant's nourishment. These physical realities, in my observation, contribute to women living in a more body-aware and body-nurturing way. They enjoy bathing, moisturizing, pedicures, and manicures. They often refer to that as pampering themselves and take full joy in it. Men, on the other hand, generally learn early on to use their bodies as competitive vehicles, something to control and dominate. Feelings of vulnerability, fear, and pain are to be denied and suppressed. Being the fastest, strongest, or most agile translates into social power for boys. This mind-set follows them into manhood. In football and other sports, boys are even trained to use their bodies as weapons. Boys are not taught to nurture their bodies. On the contrary, athletes are often not only taught to endure pain and injury but are also encouraged to "play with pain."

Even massage is often frowned upon among men. It literally astonishes me how many grown men have never had a professional massage in their entire life, even men who can easily afford it. It is often considered a frivolous and unnecessary indulgence, not a modality of healing.

I find that men are less likely than women to examine their emotional lives or to try yoga, and yet they are in the greatest need of it. Most men first come to yoga through a girlfriend or spouse. Yoga terrifies men because the degree that they need to journey through a land of unfelt and even undiscovered emotions is very daunting, to say the least. Most men are deeply invested in not showing their vulnerability, their grief, or their fear. They have an immense commitment in living an illusion of being Iron Men. Why? Because men have been trained thoroughly by our society to not show emotions, which they have been taught are signs of weakness. They were taught that to show you care, to show you are in pain, and to show grief are all taboo. The social training, put simply, is "Win or die, and never let anyone see you cry." In other words, through training by society, as a gender men become mistrusting, cut off from their feelings, and even embarrassed by their more sensitive emotions.

Think back to grammar school: If a boy was being ridiculed and shamed by others and if his eyes brimmed with tears, he would be taunted by other boys for being a "girl." Being labeled a girl meant that his status as a young warrior was stripped away, and he was made to feel that he was a social failure. Even after a brutal fistfight, after getting pummeled repeatedly in the face—no tears! At no cost must he let on that he was emotionally and physically harmed. It's my observation that this social training imprints quite deeply and carries over into adulthood in unhealthy ways. We are probably aware of this to some degree. There are statistics that tell us that men are much more susceptible to heart attacks than women and that they die sooner in general due to higher levels of tension and repressed grief. Men commit suicide much more often than women do, and we all know that men commit the large majority of violent crimes including murder and other atrocities.

As a teacher on personal transformation, I have observed that it is much more difficult to work with male students than female students in the emotional aspect of this work. I believe the reason is that although it is transformative and healing, it is also emotionally revealing. Due to everything mentioned about our training by society, this releasing and revealing goes against everything men are taught. And that scares them. A lot. It is at the root of their resistance, but few are aware enough or even able to see it. Men starve emotionally because they do not know how to share their feelings with others in order to feel understood and bond in friendship as women do with one another. When misfortune strikes, women console one another, grieve together, cry together. Men, generally, would never even think of sharing these feelings with another man, much less do it. Instead, a man will sit alone and try not to cry, and he will hate himself for even wanting to. Or he will silently go drown his sorrows with the guys at a bar. Men are taught to suck it up. Well, when you suck it up, where does your pain go? It stays in your body.

Men must try to reprogram themselves to learn that everything they were taught about suppressing emotions was good and useful in times of emergency or war, but not in times of peace and friendship. To empower our relationships, especially our intimate relationships, we need to disarm ourselves. Weapons and armor empower us only for war; they do not empower us to be good fathers, husbands, or friends. We need to stop posturing around in our armor during peacetime.

This is an important part of our personal study, becoming self-aware of our emotional infrastructure, sifting through what was programmed into us and keeping what is useful, repairing what is damaged, and dispensing with what is no longer needed.

A warrior is aptly attired when going off to fight in a battle, but if the warrior wishes to conquer himself, he must first disarm and realize that both the hero and the enemy are within himself. A good martial artist learns hardness, strength, speed, and aggression, but a great martial artist also learns to surrender, soften, and yield like water when it is appropriate and becomes master of him or herself.

Strength and surrender appear to be opposites, but this is not so. It often takes the most strength to be kind, and it takes great courage to forgive. We men should celebrate our strength but also learn to take off our armor when it no longer serves us or when it prevents us from being more emotionally intimate with those we love.

> *Life is too short for us to wear our armor while having tea with dear friends. Do we even remember how to remove it? Did we forget that we are wearing it? Such precious moments with dear friends—so few of them.*

THE OVERCOMPENSATION SYNDROME

So many of us do not feel that we make a difference, so we try to make an impression.

This is particularly evident with teenagers as they attempt to socially define themselves through tribal-specific clothing and other bodily accoutrements, striving hard to belong and to simultaneously stand out. Piercings, tattoos, and shocking haircuts and color are all attempts to escape a sense of invisibility, which feels not just like disempowerment but more as if walking through the streets like a phantom. Though this syndrome is usually the most obvious with teenagers, today the same, now rampant, syndrome seems to be carried by people into their thirties, forties, and beyond. Their tribal prestige badges are different from their teenagers', with their status being represented by culture-specific automobiles and brand-name handbags, but the symptoms reveal the same need—to belong and simultaneously to stand out. It is not unlikely that this phenomenon has been exacerbated in part due to the disempowerment we feel in our hyperchanging environment. We desperately want, whether we know it or not, to feel that we are being seen clearly.

We all fall victim to this need, but to truly become self-aware we must study ourselves in this way. Perhaps we must stop trying to be what we think people want us to be, and finally show people who we truly are, because that is how both our power and our happiness come to be.

Take a moment of self-reflection and make a list of the ways that you strive to belong and to simultaneously stand out using visual symbols to do so. Include clothing, bodily accoutrements, slanguage, and possessions as well. No one needs to see this list but you. But it is crucial that *you* see it and that you understand how this behavior is symptomatic behavior of an emotional need. Once you have your list, ask yourself whether if you stopped using these symbols those whom you respect the most would care. What would happen to your relationships? You my find that it would indeed negatively impact a few of your relationships, but these may just be the relationships that are holding you back from fulfilling your true mission in this life. Conversely, by letting go of the host of symbolic social messages you send through your physical persona and so on, you may find that you now attract people whom you have not attracted before and who will see you as you truly are, and want to be your friend as a result.

Grief is such a powerful emotion, and I dare say that it is the emotion that we are the most frightened to feel. When a tragedy strikes, many will do everything they can to avoid the feelings of grief that are exploding in their chest. Some try and cover their feelings with anger and even convert their anger to vengeance. Others will shut down as if feeling nothing. And still others will move into action to try to fix the situation, to fix the unfixable, or to create solutions to prevent another similar tragedy from ever happening again. In all three cases, the grief is suppressed. Buried. But grief demands its moment, its time. We all need to embrace our grief and let it purify us. But we fear grief so much that many powerful warriors would gladly go into an unwinnable battle and feel a bullet enter their chest rather than feel their own grief. This is because we often believe that our grief would destroy us when fully experienced, that we could not survive. In many cultures, men are taught that to allow yourself to collapse in grief means a complete failure as a man or that you are now irrelevant. We see no good in it—only indescribable pain. I believe that grief does offer gifts, and one powerful gift is the gift of piercing clarity. Grief is like a cold blue flame that burns away everything to its essence until you are overtaken by the harsh clarity of who you really are as an emotional being. You are in full witness of your wounds, your strengths, and your failures. It also gives you, for a time, a special kind of vision, a vision of true love, a vision that cuts through everything except that which is absolutely true, revealing the one you love the most fiercely in the depth of your bones. You see the correlation of love and those of your friends and family you feel comfortable sharing your grief with. In other words, you realize whom you truly have an intimate relationship with and with whom you do not. In my darkest hours of extreme grief, these were the things that I could clearly witness. Love stripped bare. The intensity of grief can be nearly unbearable. It can feel as if your heart is being crushed and your breath is being sucked into a black hole within. Our lungs convulse in spasms, and to inhale can be almost impossible. We have all felt this intensity, usually from the loss of a loved one to bodily death or due to the permanent demise of a relationship. But grief can also erupt from the loss of our own innocence and from our perception that we have failed those who depend on us, who need us. There are many causes of grief; there are even times when we grieve for the moral failings of mankind.

I believe that the reason why grief can be so intensely over-whelming is that it is the reaction of two absolute forces collid-ing. For example, someone whom you love wholeheartedly has died without warning, someone whom you would protect at almost any cost. Now that beloved has suddenly been ripped from your life. Your shock quickly transmutes into grief, a grief that debilitates you like no other emotion. The two absolute forces collide—one force is your absolute committed love and attachment to this person, and the other force is the absolute permanence of death. The two equally absolute forces colliding shatter your heart because they are irrecon-cilable, and the conflicted emotions we feel are the root of our grief.

The grief pervades your daily life until you find a way to reconcile these two forces. In the case of a death, death will always prevail. The reconciliation can happen in only one way, when you finally come to accept the new order of things, a life without the physical presence of your beloved.

Another factor that can make grief so intense is that there is almost always grief beneath the grief. Previously repressed grief lies deeper within you than the new grief, and when you allow the new grief to be experienced and processed, it is followed by your older buried grief; like a tidal wave it rises and surges through your body as an unstoppable catharsis. As I mentioned before, it can be a powerful purification, perhaps the most important one of your life, leaving you with a strong sense of a new direction or absolute clarification of what choices must now be taken with regard to your key relationships and your life. After the storm, you receive a precious knowledge, real and beyond all doubt. The grieving process slowly subsides as you gradually surrender to the absolute, to what is, and you accept what cannot be changed. But this cannot be rushed.

If we try to hurry the process of grief, very often what can happen is we simply repress it, storing it once again deep within our body, unhealed. This is why during a time of grief it is important to stay close with those who are not afraid of grief and can be supportive in your process without hurrying you or judging you and in front of whom you feel comfortable weeping or breaking down.

The only way out of grief is through it.

Stay close to those who do not impose their philosophical or religious views of death upon you or try to persuade you that what happened to cause the grief was a positive thing. For example, when a small child dies, telling the parent immersed in grief that "God wanted your child to be an angel in Heaven" is presumably meant with love, but this kind of imposing life view can feel brutally callous to the bereaved parent. The parent might then simply become angry with God. What is more likely to be comforting to the parents is for them to know that you are there for them and that you grieve with them.

Stay close to those who understand that grief can cause irrational behavior and will allow for that. For example, when someone passes away, it may console the bereaved to sit in the deceased's room and hold something that was an intimate object of the deceased. Accept that as part of the process of the grieving; do not try to discourage it. For someone to unclench his or her hands and release the physical presence of the deceased beloved takes some time.

If it is you who is in the presence of someone overwhelmed with grief, do not look away or avoid that person's heartbroken glance. Do not fear grief; it is one of the most potent bridges between human beings. My wife told me the story of how when she was leaving a veterinarian's office one day, she observed a woman at the front desk with an empty pet case in her hand and tears staining her cheeks. It was obvious that the woman had just watched her pet be euthanized and was now trying to finish up the paperwork as she held her grief in check for a few moments. My wife, having had the same sorrowful experience some months before with her own pet, was moved by the woman with the empty case. She walked over to her and gently clasped her hand for just a moment. The woman turned, and they met eyes for a second, just a moment of mutual understanding, empathy, and compassion. They gave each other a small reassuring nod and then, without a word spoken, walked away. She says she still vividly remembers the woman's eyes and their connection.

If a friend is grieving and sharing their story with you, never, ever, change the subject. The subject should only be changed by the person who is grieving. If the friend is sharing their grief with you it shows that they trust you and feel a certain amount of intimacy with you. For you to change the subject indicates that either you cannot sympathize with him or her, or that you do not wish to have this level of intimacy. You are in a sense quite vigorously pushing that person away.

To be of help to the grieving, you do not need wise words, only a fearless heart and a kindness in your eyes. You can hold someone and say nothing and be a great help. All you need is to give your warm presence for a moment and to show that you understand and sincerely care and that there is room for the person's grief in this world. Though fierce in its power, the catharsis of grief can ultimately be the great healer, one of the most powerful, and like having survived a nearly fatal fever, at some point you awaken from it renewed and even reborn.

CULTIVATING INTIMACY

To increase the quality of our daily lives, we need to increase the quality of our intimate relationships. Intimacy is one of the most vital pillars of our social structure, yet it seems that until very recently it was also one of the most misunderstood aspects of human relationships.

In the first half of the twentieth century, parents were advised by experts never to pick up a crying infant for fear of spoiling him. It was later understood that this was misguided (if not cruel), that babies need to be held regularly, and that they will cry to communicate this need.

Adults also need human contact. Think for a moment about how prisoners are punished for violence in a penitentiary—they are put in solitary confinement. Human beings hate solitary confinement. To be alienated from a social community, to not hear, see, or touch other humans, can drive a person to the point of insanity. Some call it "social-sensory deprivation syndrome," and it is a common method of torture.

Now we are unconsciously removing ourselves from this physical or visceral intimacy as we stare at the flat screen in its place. We all need actual, not virtual, human physical presence and touch. We need the voices and even scent of our loved ones. We are wired for it. It is our bodies that experience and communicate our emotions, and that is why our relationships are mostly nonverbal. I have strong doubts that companion bots and sex androids will fill this very real need for community. I believe that the need for bonding with humans will be just as relevant in the future as it is now.

I recently had a conversation in which we were discussing the perceived value of an autographed signature. We all know that many people readily desire the autograph of a person whom they hold in esteem, such as an athlete, politician, author, or artist. It is not uncommon for people to wait long periods of time for a celebrity to sign a photograph or book, or for a sports hero to sign a ball.

There is such value placed on the celebrity autographs that there is a vibrant collector's market. Sports memorabilia signed by a whole team can sometimes be sold for hundreds or thousands of dollars.

An autograph, or better yet, a photo of you standing next to the celebrity, proves contact with the notable person—that you were actually in his or her presence, had a conversation, and looked in each other's eyes. It was an achieved moment of intimacy, no matter how brief. We hold these moments in high regard, framing the autographed photo and placing it prominently on the wall, or placing an autographed baseball in the glass case. The autograph is a symbol of intimate contact and cannot be replaced by a virtual autograph. In fact, the virtual autograph is considered a forgery and has little or no value. This is a perfect example of the difference between the actual and the virtual, the personal and the impersonal, or the intimate and the alienated. This is why a hand-written card or letter is far more valuable now than it has ever been before, since so many of us now send virtual cards and letters or emails in their stead. Many of us have lost our sense of appropriateness for such things and even habitually send congratulatory messages, thank-you notes, or holiday greetings via text messaging. There is no substitute for the actual human presence of those we love or admire. This will perhaps never change, and I doubt seriously that we will become collectors of text messages. What do you think?

The physical expression of emotions is easy to see in everyday life. If you sit on a park bench on a busy day and watch people passing by, you can see which children belong to whom by the body language of both the adults and the children. Is she the mother or a baby sitter? It is usually quite obvious. You can see a man in his forties walking with a man in his sixties, both in business suits, and you can tell whether they are business associates or father and son. You can see two other people walking together and know if they are lovers simply by the nonverbal body language even when they are not touching one another. You will see families walking together and perceive if they are close or estranged from each other. You can see all of this via nonverbal communication. It's in the body language and the nuances of facial expression.

Many of us had very difficult childhoods, or worse, traumatic ones, and we had no infrastructure or context to process what was happening, so we put up our shields. The shield, or armor, can include body language that can portray toughness or simply send nonverbal signals to stay away, such as facial expressions that repel others or are intently neutral, with avoidance of eye contact. The way we dress sometimes reflects an intention to keep people from approaching us rather than create a sense of openness. Some of us will acquire a manner of speech that is fierce or laced with profanities. We think that this shows strength, but these kinds of clothing or verbal tactics serve to conceal our fear. Safety trumps loneliness. But these habits of shielding were learned in childhood and carried well into adulthood, and we forget that they even exist. When they are pointed out to us, we feel a powerful knee-jerk resistance. For example, when it is suggested that we alter our clothing or hair for more approachability to better our chances of employment, we may feel anxiety at the prospect of changing "our style." The sum total of these subconscious tactics makes us unapproachable to others and can greatly contribute to our loneliness and even create problems of truly connecting in what we think are intimate relationships.

Here is a different but equally common example of subconscious shielding. A woman, whom we'll call Marcia, doesn't dress to repel—quite the contrary—but her body language is like barbed wire. We have all seen people like Marcia at parties, standing alone with a drink in hand, who have clearly taken a great deal of time getting ready to make themselves attractive through makeup, hair, and ensemble, yet their body language says, *Stay away.* At the party, Marcia's body posture subconsciously takes on a defiant stance, and her facial expression is a blend of near-disgust and smugness. Marcia hates gatherings like these because she is reminded that people do not notice her. She feels invisible and that people do not like her. But it isn't that people do not notice her or like her; it is actually through subconscious, nonverbal tactics that she is essentially telling people to keep away from her. Intimacy is one of our greatest fears. We all think we want it, but we don't want to look into anyone's eyes to get it. I'm not talking only about physical intimacy but also about human intimacy, from friendship to partnership and family.

The following allegory explains the situation and the purpose of our work. Imagine a nearly dark room. A human being is like a lit candle in that room, covered by a basket. The candle symbolizes your inner light, your soul, and the basket symbolizes everything with which you cover your soul in an attempt to protect yourself. We all are born with the same amount of light, but others can see only a little flickering of your light through the weaving of the basket. Your work is to remove the basket, piece by piece, in order to reveal all of your light, your authentic power, and help illuminate this world.

What is counterintuitive about this allegory is that by removing the basket, your protection, you actually become more powerful. Normally, we do not think of power as gained by release and surrender but by fighting and acquiring. In this case, true power is gained through exposure and vulnerability. You cannot shield yourself from adversaries only; a shield does not discriminate between friendship and malice; it keeps everyone out. But by removing the basket, power is gained by allowing people to get closer to your heart so that your relationships grow deeper and richer and your constant loneliness is extinguished. When this happens, your craving and clinging to shreds of intimacy decrease, and you find yourself living in a healthier and very real family and community. Your self-worth soars, and because you are no longer struggling in alienation, you begin to gain a wisdom that you did not have before, and your choices improve exponentially.

The Courage of Vulnerability

We have a bright light within us, with which we are meant to shine out into this world, and we can become brighter still by removing the armor that is covering our light. Courage is what we need to take our own armor off, and courage is what we sometimes need to keep others from covering our light.

Because of the heartbreaking experiences that life provides us with, we tend to protect our hearts by building walls around them. I speak of this often and refer to it as armor. But what is this armor? Symbolically speaking, imagine your heart encased in ice, the ice being frozen emotions such as grief, betrayal, rage, and disappointment. In our attempt to guard our hearts, we subconsciously keep people whom we truly want to be close with at a distance, then we wonder what their problem is. Why do they stay at arms length? Why do people always leave us? To have a life that includes meaningful intimacy, we must find the courage to melt the ice wall and expose our hearts to the world. This act terrifies many of us because it seems dangerously vulnerable and we may feel like a snail without its shell. Based on our heart being shattered before, we dare not expose it again. This is why the process requires some degree of conscious work in opening the heart center—every day—choosing to reveal the light within and receive the light and love of others. We cannot expect a radical change to happen overnight. We all had good reasons to shield ourselves as children or teenagers, and our shield mechanisms are deeply entrenched. Exposing your heart does not mean to live without wisdom, boundaries, or discernment. It does not mean that you turn into a doormat or become instantly vulnerable with people who seem untrustworthy, but it does mean *you* must take the first step to melt the shield. And it is this initial step that is the hardest.

I remember a similar experience from my childhood. Born with clubbed feet, I spent many years of my early life in plaster casts and braces. Often I was put in casts for periods of six weeks. By the time the cast came off, my leg size and strength had diminished, and the itching caused from the cotton wrapping beneath the plaster was nearly intolerable. In short, I couldn't wait for the cast to come off. On the big day, the doctor would use a special electric saw to cut it off, and after a few unpleasant minutes, I was liberated. But I have to tell you, my initial feeling of the cast coming off was very unpleasant and a little scary. The saw sometimes hurt a little, so the process itself was frightening to a small boy, but when my leg was exposed to the air, it felt cold, raw, and vulnerable. The skin, having been heavily insulated for six weeks, was not used to the "cold" outside temperature. My first inclination was to cover my leg again. I had to push past these feelings because, after cleaning the leg and foot, in a little while, my leg, although weaker, began to feel better.

The process of revealing your inner self might be a little painful, and the first feelings of exposing your heart to others may also feel cold, raw, and very vulnerable. And that is when you are faced with a choice; you have to choose whether to keep the wall down or to put the wall back up. If you use your courage and keep the wall down, in a while, your heart will feel better than ever as it breathes new life force into it, and it is allowed to shine brighter into the world.

The more we learn about how to take off our armor and choose to be authentic, the more we transform from masked strangers into lighthouses.

What helped me remove the ice armor that I used to wear was the breathing practices. I went through a period in my life when I didn't cry for ten years or longer. Even while watching a very sad movie, you would not see a tear on my face. I was very shut down in this way. But through yoga and especially the breathing work, it all started cracking open, like a shell cracking apart. The shell around the heart center released and gave birth to forgiveness and compassion. Now, if I watch a sad movie with my wife, sometimes she hands me a tissue in advance. It doesn't take much to bring tears forth from my heart. Most of the ice armor has been removed. This was from the work, and the work must continue a little every day.

If you integrate the first imperative, self-study, into your daily life, you will begin to dissolve old behaviors and open up your shields energetically. People will notice a change in you that they cannot describe, and you will appear much more approachable and friendly.

Exercises:

- Practice speaking about your emotions, especially love, in a direct and kind way, telling your loved ones how you feel, and when people say they love you, never deflect it with jokes or space-fillers, just make eye contact, smile genuinely, and take it in.

- Because most people do not feel heard, if you want intimacy, you must become a great listener first. Learn to make eye contact so that you are 100 percent present for those with whom you are communicating.

- Intimacy is supported by healthy and clear communication. To communicate well, you must learn to inspire with your spoken words; however simple, they can always be heartfelt and respectful. To improve your speaking skills and language is to improve your intimacy; one is not without the other. Your emotional intention fills your body with emotional power, and that power brings to life your words that can never be obtained with words alone. Read Martin Luther King's "I Have a Dream" speech, and it is moving, but hear it, and it can be life changing. The voice carries the emotional power of the words. A living voice is more powerful than the written voice, and seeing the eyes of the speaker can takes us to the depth of the speaker's soul and sometimes to the depths of our own souls too.

- Fully acknowledging people, even for sixty seconds, can be very powerful. I have a saying: "Every time we speak, we have an opportunity to change the world." And we do. *But we have to be fully present when we speak.* When you look at someone, make sure you are 100 percent present for him or her.

- To learn to be with others, you must gradually learn to be alone. You must overcome the fear of solitude or silence. You will accomplish this following the first and third imperatives.

RESPECT: IT FEELS JUST LIKE LOVE

Another way to cultivate more intimacy in your life is by showing authentic respect toward others. I think people misunderstand this because they learned the meaning of respect in a scolding manner from their parents, such as, "You will show me respect, young lady!" or that sort of thing. In that scenario, respect can be easily confused with submission. The respect that I am referring to is not submission but a clear acknowledgment to another human being that you regard his or her existence and well-being. Showing genuine respect fosters intimacy as it causes people to begin to trust you as well as respect you in return. Being shown respect feels very similar to affection, and even love. This is because it is a form of love. When someone is treated disrespectfully, it feels like indifference, the absence of love. For example, have you ever had someone say something like this to you in a heated discussion: "You say you love me, but how could you love me if you speak to me in that tone?!" When someone is disrespectful to us, it usually makes us question the depth of love that person feels for us. Again, love feels like respect, and respect feels like love. If you show disrespect, people begin to believe that you do not love them or perhaps even regard them at all. Disrespect is a form of violence.

Using this in the context of interacting with people outside the home, notice how a man will make a purchase from a store clerk while talking on his cell phone. The unspoken message to the clerk is: "I disrespect you. You're 'just a cashier,' and so I have no regard for you." And then the man on the cell phone wonders why he feels lonely. It's because he is treating most people around him with disrespect. It's little things like that. But there are no little things.

RESPECT IN THE WORKPLACE

Respect is an essential component not only to our personal lives but also in the workplace. It is my contention that showing respect to coworkers, employees, and employers is not only the right thing to do, or the kind thing to do, but it is actually the most profitable thing to do. Let's look at a common corporate concern, employee retention. Employee retention, in plain language, is measured by the fewest number of employees that resign on their own account. In the business world, a significant priority of employers is to decrease employee turnover. This is important because when you decrease employee turnover, you decrease training costs. This is meaningful beyond money spent, and it is also costly in terms of performance. A seasoned, experienced worker is far more efficient than someone who has just been trained and is still green. Decreasing employee turnover also decreases the loss of good leaders and unique knowledge of the inner workings of the business. Businesses, especially corporations, spend a lot of time and money creating tactics to retain employees by offering reward systems. But what I have seen commonly overlooked is the simple, inexpensive practice of showing respect to your employees. If retention is your company's strategy, then showing and feeling respect for your employees is critical.

At a recent conference I gave in the Washington, D. C. area, I was lecturing on ethics in business and asked for a show of hands on this issue. I said, "I have witnessed a trend where some corporations take good care of their upper echelon executives, and they take great care of their customers, but they nickel-and-dime and abuse their staff. Raise your hand if you have seen this and agree that this is a problem." You should have seen the hands shoot up and the groans of frustrated agreement. In that room of professionals and spouses of professionals, I had touched on a hot topic. To this same group I then told this story:

This was relayed to me from a businesswoman I know; we'll call her Rachel. Rachel is smart, organized, motivated, and friendly. She worked for a successful business with over forty employees as the general manager and was efficient and well liked. A Madison Avenue corporation then acquired the business. One afternoon, the CEO and a few other team members came in from New York to their new acquisition. The CEO spent a few hours looking things over, meeting the entire staff, shaking hands, etc.—the usual scenario of a first-time official visit. Rachel was a little nervous about meeting the CEO and did not have an opportunity to have an actual conversation. The CEO, let's call her Mrs. Jones, was a very busy woman. She was all too frequently on her hand-held device and constantly ran late for meetings. In her meetings, she rushed through her agenda and was not known for being a good listener. When she was ready to leave Rachel's location and go back to her hotel, Mrs. Jones turned to Rachel and asked her to call a taxi for her. Rachel took the opportunity to try to have at least a few minutes to get to know her new employer. So, Rachel said that she would be happy to drive Mrs. Jones to the hotel. But while in the car, Mrs. Jones immediately went onto her Smartphone and made some quick calls. There was no conversation whatsoever with Rachel in the ten-minute drive. Rachel was embarrassed that Mrs. Jones showed no interest, made no eye contact, and uttered not a single word to her in the car. When they pulled up to the entrance of the hotel, the CEO, Mrs. Jones, continued talking on her phone as she climbed out of the car, closed the door, and headed into the hotel. She did not say "thank you" and did not make eye contact but simply got out of the car and walked away as if getting off a train. Rachel was humiliated.

I then asked the conference group in front of me, "What did Rachel do next?" Almost in unison several people called out, "She started planning her exit strategy." And that was exactly what she did. Now, you may be thinking that Mrs. Jones knew that she was going to replace Rachel and that is why she wasn't friendly. But that is not what happened; Rachel was kept in her management position. There was no plan to let her go. But the CEO, Mrs. Jones, in one ten-minute car ride, through nonverbal communication, made Rachel feel disrespected, unseen, and insignificant. And this was all it took for Rachel to know that she didn't want to work for that company.

Disrespect toward your employees creates low job satisfaction and thereby decreases retention. Speaking to and behaving in a respectful way creates loyalty, good will, and motivation.

A poor leader can manage people by the stick. A better leader uses the carrot and the stick. The greatest leaders, who champion a cause larger than themselves and who show respect to others, need no stick at all.

RESPECT IN THE PRACTICE ROOM

Behaving with respect in the room where we practice breath-initiated movement, yoga, or chi gung is so very important. Showing respect is a form of kindness. In the world of martial arts, respect is of immense importance probably because opponents know that they can kill each other. By adhering to a strict code of respect, they're essentially saying, "I respect you. I'll be careful with you because I know what we're doing is very dangerous, and we're taking each other's lives into our hands. I respect your practice enough to trust you and watch out for your safety." I think in yoga the concept of respect needs to be brought more to light, as respect is a way to show love toward each other.

At one of my retreats years ago, we had a fire circle on the last night where each person took turns speaking. It was the evening of New Year's Day, 2000. Someone had commented to my dear friend and assistant, John Hogan, that he had noticed how silent John was in his entry and exit from the practice room. His presence was never a distraction. He answered this student by saying, "The reason I'm so careful to not disturb you is because I know how hard it is to get on that mat and pull yourselves open every day. And I respect each and every one of you for this enough to try my hardest not to disturb you when I come in the door, and when I leave, to leave quietly so that you would never know that I was there. The only sound I want you to hear from me is the sound of my breath."

Exercises of Respect:

1. To foster respectful behavior to others, fully acknowledge people when speaking to them. Offer a sincere smile and be totally present, even in a brief conversation, even for thirty seconds. This can have a very powerful effect.

2. Make a list of ten things that people do that make you feel respected. Keep the list in your pocket or handbag until you memorize those behaviors and begin to use them in your relationships, treating others the way you would want to be treated.

3. Ask yourself if there is anyone in your life that you may be taking for granted. Reexamine why it is that you may show the least amount of respect to those who love you the most and great respect to those who do not treat you well.

Showing Respect in Business:

1. Pay your bills on time; if there is a delay beyond your control, communicate that you are sorry and you are making extra efforts to fix it. Paying bills promptly is unusual and will make you stand out as a respectful and trustworthy business.

2. If your company causes a problem, take responsibility, apologize, and communicate what steps you have taken to fix it, then follow up until it is right. Do it quickly—speed connotes importance.

3. Return calls and emails promptly; again, speed connotes importance. Include personal greetings. It only takes seconds and is a way of reestablishing connection every time.

4. Show up to meetings (and meals) a few minutes early. If you are running late, call, apologize, and communicate your ETA. Never cancel a meeting at the last minute unless there is an actual emergency.

5. If you intend to pay for lunch, take care of it in advance. (This isn't difficult when you arrive early.) By paying in advance before your lunch partner arrives, you will avoid the dance of who grabs the check quickest or an awkward discussion on who paid last. It makes the bill-paying process seamless and graceful and expresses your intention with absolute clarity. It really feels like a gift, not a negotiation.

Again, to be shown respect feels like you are cared for and that you are valued. Your time is you, so if someone values your time, he or she values you. Lack of respect causes people to feel like you do not value them or care about them—even if you do. In their hearts they then redesignate the relationship with you as business only, and they will no longer give you the benefit of the doubt or look out for you. And that is exactly what you deserve in this case. So, in essence, by showing disrespect, you are creating a world where people who did like you no longer do. You are the cause of loss of friendship and trust, and you are slowly alienating yourself from good, ethical people with healthy boundaries.

Every meaningful relationship needs trust, respect, and affection or love. Without one of these, the relationship is wounded and will disintegrate.

RESPECT AND BLOGGING

Blogging is arguably one of the new gifts to free speech and democracy, as it offers a place for everyone to be read or heard. However, so many comments on blogs are condescending and quite often even malicious that blogging has become one of the most disrespectful offshoots of the tech revolution. It is now commonplace for those making critical comments to attack the writer personally, hurling adjectives like "moron," "idiot," etc. The unbridled maelstrom of words I have seen is astonishing to me. Some seem to clearly enjoy the process of lacerating the author of the article as if, metaphorically, having knocked him down, they then proceed to repeatedly kick him in the face. This seems to be becoming, sadly, the new accepted standard. Of course, people who comment with hostility almost always use a code name. I suspect that anonymous blogging motivates people who feel unheard to overcompensate and become verbal cyber bullies, with the resulting name-calling. Communicating criticism to someone you have never met, via text and hidden behind a veil of anonymity, clearly perpetuates the worst in us.

I recall the axiom, "Never assume you know the inner motivations of a person. Therefore, never criticize the person; criticize the behavior." I believe this is a most wise piece of advice. I am reminded of how a teenager often cannot distinguish between a person's behavior and the person. An angered teenager may shout at his parents, "I hate you!" and mean it in the moment, only to realize later that he indeed loves his parents. I believe that it's an indication that someone has matured into an adult by this very ability to distinguish between these two things—a person and the person's behavior. Only a mature adult can say and mean, "I love you, but I am angry with you." So, in context to blogging, when I read cruel and bitter personal attacks, what I see is perhaps someone who has yet to mature to this point—someone who hates a behavior and so feels hatred toward the person.

I would like to suggest that blogs institute their own new guidelines so that comments can no longer be anonymous and that we must from now on list our legal name along with a two-sentence bio. If blogs would also implement software that would filter out profanities, this might be the beginning of a return to civility. I ask all of you who comment on blogs to write your criticisms without personal disparagements. Learn to express yourself and your ideas and deep beliefs without insulting those who think and feel differently. Critique the actions and behavior, not the man or woman. This is the next step into adulthood and the kind of society we all strive for. If we want a world of peace and humanity, we must first concern ourselves with what comes forth from the thoughts in our heads to our fingertips touching the keyboard.

To summarize, self-study leads to self-awareness so you can see yourself clearly in as many aspects as possible. It is simple: The higher degree of self-awareness you achieve, the better choices you will make on your life path. Happiness, as defined by the daily experience of a meaningful life, comes as a culmination of self-knowledge integrated with the second and third imperatives. This is why self-awareness is such an important step, an imperative to passionately embark upon.

Self-knowledge is power.

IMPERATIVE 2:
LIVE AS IF YOUR TIME AND YOUR
LIFE SPAN WERE THE SAME THING

The Imperative of Life-Span Management

Your time and your life span are the same thing. But we have an incongruous schism between the concepts of our time and our life span, at our own peril. What you spend your time on is what you spend your life on. But many of us think of the concepts of *time* and *life* as two completely separate things. In one hand we have a precious short life, and in the other hand we have time to kill. Time is not only money, it is far more than that; it is the minutes and seconds of your mortal life. Your time is the finite resource from which you experience this world, everyone, everything, and especially that which you are devoted to and live for. Time consists in the precious moments to which we so dearly cling.

It has been said that the most epic illusion mankind has about itself is the illusion of earthly immortality, that we will never die. But when reality has proven the contrary by around age forty, when our first major aging symptoms become undeniable and we recognize that our bodies will grow old and die, the split between *time* and *life span* really takes hold. Recognizing that our bodies are aging, we may soberly begin to plan for our retirement, purchase life insurance, and even create a detailed will and testament. We start taking supplements, try dieting, and take blood-thinning medicine to ward off the possibility of stroke or heart attack. But that is all aimed at our life span, not our time. Where our time is concerned, we continue to behave as if we were nearly immortal.

To illustrate this, all we need to do is remember the aforementioned Gothenburg study that found that among young Facebook users, two-thirds claimed they used the site to kill time.

Two more examples:

According to a recent study by Performance Research, nationwide NASCAR fans can be described as predominately employed, married forty-two-year-old men. NASCAR events are so popular that they can fill stadiums with a quarter of a million people at around $80 per person, all gathered to, in essence, watch cars driving around in circles at high speeds.

Television viewing for people over sixty-five averages forty-eight hours a week, or nearly seven hours a day, says a 2011 Nielsen report.

Examples like these indicate that although people over forty plan their finances around aging and the eventuality of bodily death, they spend an incredible amount of their increasingly limited life span "killing time."

BARTERING YOUR TIME

Our mortal time is a finite resource, so whether we are aware of it or not, we all purchase each time-event at the cost of another.

> A time-event is what I call a specialized event, such as a business meeting, playing a video game, going out on a date, or watching your child's soccer game.

Once you have begun your journey of self-awareness and you have reprioritized your daily schedule, the next step is to barter time-events that are not useful to you any longer in exchange for time-events that will elicit more happiness and meaning. For example, two decades ago I used to watch NFL football each and every season. One autumn, I felt that I wanted to find more time in my life to read and study. My intention was to allocate at least five hours of study time each week, but I couldn't really see where I would find the time. One day, while reading the sports page, I came to realize exactly where I could find it. It came to me that during football season I generally watched two games a week

(3.2 hours per game, including commercials), and I read about football in the sports page an additional two hours a week. On top of that, I talked football with friends an additional one hour per week. In total, I spent around nine hours per week on football. Although I enjoyed the game, I really wanted to deepen my study, as I was inspired to continue on the path of renewal I had begun. It became obvious that football was ultimately not bringing me any kind of fulfillment; it was simply entertainment and nothing more. Not that entertainment is wrong, but it was costing me too much time and was thus too expensive. So, I made a trade. I traded all nine hours of football per week in exchange for about five hours of reading, and I had an additional four hours a week left over to use for personal time. I have never regretted that trade for a second.

Nine hours per week on football = 144 hours per season. Over a period of sixty years, this would come to a minimum 8,640 hours of my life.

What is stealing your time? Calculate that here.

We have to make sacrifices to have a fulfilling life. Happiness costs something. What are you willing to sacrifice? To decide what you are willing to sacrifice, first determine what you think of as your most precious things. What makes your life worth living? Often it is our family and their health, well-being, and safety. The joy of our children, the majesty of our natural world, ocean, sky, forest, desert, and mountains. The awesome beauty of the animal kingdom. Our own bodies in a state of health and vitality. Our spiritual hearts in accord with their source. Our access to knowledge and justice and humanity's finest art. We all make our own list when we suspect that we will be leaving this world—this is when what is of true value grows brighter and what is not recedes from our vision. None of those who are nearing death ask for their monetary net worth to be placed on their headstone, because at that point they know how little it means.

Real versus Perceived Value

Most of us believe that it is money that will make us happy; even though many of us have money now and are not happy, yet strangely we still believe it. Examine real versus perceived value. What truly adds value to your life? For example, do you remember the five happiest and most meaningful days in your life? (Not including your wedding or the birth of your children.) As you envision the five happiest days, how much did money have to do with the beauty and wonder of those days? Most likely, very little.

> *My favorite things in life don't cost any money. It's really clear that the most precious resource we all have is time.*
>
> ~ Steve Jobs

I am sharing this quote not because it is unique, because it isn't. Similar quotes have been made by wise people for eons. I share this particular quote because these words were spoken by a businessman who was an icon of success, not a saint. Steve Jobs achieved great wealth, power, and fame, only to discover that his favorite things in life were free.

If you want to increase your life span, do it by increasing the quality of your hours, increase the hours you spend doing things you love and helping others. When you help, educate, heal, or nurture other people, your days become more and more meaningful, and you enrich the quality of your hours. This is a different way of thinking, you have to train for it—train your mind to think differently.

Exercise: Bartering Your Time

1. Track your time—learn how you're spending it now. Write down what you're doing every day for one week. Keep a journal or do a spreadsheet.

2. Now that you have your one-week tracking complete, you will understand truly how you allocate your time. Now, list your activities by priority. What activities are crucial financially, physically, and of course, emotionally? Take a second look at the emotional list because it is likely that you underschedule some activities, such as quiet time with your family, reading, or exercise, and overschedule other things, like passive entertainment, gaming, Facebooking, etc.

3. Now that you have reevaluated your priorities, you will need to shift some things around. Since each day is limited to twenty-four hours, you will have to eliminate, or massively shrink, some activities to make room for expanding more significant activities, such as following a new regime that brings a deeper level of fulfillment to your spouse, your children, and yourself. The next step is to find bartering opportunities. Example: I will trade ____ hours of my_____ in order to use that time to_____.

4. Schedule your daily practice rather than wait for openings in your busy schedule. (Your daily practice will be covered thoroughly in the section discussing the third imperative.)

5. Schedule everything that is important to you up to a year in advance. This feels totally bizarre for many people. Because I travel so often, I have to schedule my life up to two years

in advance. When I first tried doing this, it was very difficult psychologically. That many commitments over that length of time were far beyond my comfort level. But after doing it, I found it extremely beneficial in unforeseen ways as it continually caused me to stand back and look at my life and plan in two-year increments. And rather than making me less aware of the moments in my life, it brought me more deeply into them.

6. Become a collector of free time versus busy time. Schedule in time for which you have no plans. Have entire weekends with no plans. Book a vacation in Paris with no itinerary once you get there. Bumble around and feel what it is like to live spontaneously. When I visited India, I studied my guidebook carefully, noting the hotels that seemed best suited for my needs. But then one day a friend of mine made a gentle suggestion; she said, "Millions of people are reading the same guidebook. I suggest you book a hotel for the first few days you arrive to settle in, and after that, allow yourself to discover places to stay, eat, etc., that are not in the book." This advice was invaluable, and I have found it applies to life in general here at home, not just in India. Getting out into nature is also an integral part of our practice. Whether it's for a few minutes of breathing, meditation, a brisk walk, or a movement session, nature nourishes your energy system and connects you to the timeless source.

MANAGING YOUR LIFE SPAN: COMMITMENT INTEGRITY

This section is for those who suffer and/or create suffering in others through time mismanagement and the neglect of commitments.

Your time is your life span; to lack control of your time is to lack control of your life. Running late is often referred to as a time management issue, but try thinking of it as *life span management* and *commitment integrity*. It has impact on many areas of your life but especially on your relationships. Your ability to arrive and depart according to your commitments is one of the ways people ascertain if they can rely on you or if they will respect you. I used to be a late person many years ago. I habitually ran late to both business and social commitments until I was about thirty-five years old. I ran an average of twenty minutes late and would nearly always feel stress and guilt from doing so, and I would do this almost every day. The pivotal event that caused me to seriously reassess this negative habit was when I ran a full hour late to what was, at that time, the most important business meeting of my life. Upon arriving to the meeting, I was so stressed, embarrassed, and angry with myself that there was no other way I could interpret what happened other than call it a clear case of self-sabotage. The surface cause of my lateness was that I had not accounted for heavy traffic on a route I had never driven. In other words, I did not prepare whatsoever for things going wrong on the roadways in Los Angeles en route to the most important and potentially beneficial meeting that could influence the course of my career. I was saved from humiliation and damage to my career as the man who called the meeting was running five minutes later than I was. But after that humiliating event, I vowed to change my ways and end the cycle of stress and guilt.

In my case, my habit of running late was a form of self-sabotage as it caused me to suffer as well as inconvenience those waiting for me. But for some people the cause of this issue is different. I know someone, for example, who is chronically late, but it causes no stress in her whatsoever. Running late may be a passive-aggressive way of controlling those around you. But whatever the cause of your late-ness, there is always damage done to others and to yourself. I have noticed that with only a few exceptions, it is the most successful and busiest business people I know who are almost always the first to arrive to my workshops. In other words, those with the busiest, most complex, and high-pressure careers, who have the best excuses for running late, understand the value of promptness and live by it.

Here are some of the common excuses and myths for running late:

- I don't want to interrupt the flow of what is going on, such as a great conversation.
- I can't stand arriving early and having nothing to do.
- I don't remember to plan out how much time it actually takes me to get somewhere.
- People really don't mind so much if I'm late. The only peo-ple who mind are people with control issues; so it's their problem, not mine.

- I am very spiritual and am concerned with higher things.

What you may be unaware of:

- You have probably lost friends over this issue and are not aware of it because they did not tell you.
- You have definitely lost business because of it.
- Most people resent and are offended by being kept waiting. They feel like you do not respect or care about them. Or it makes them not trust you.
- People feel that if you are unreliable in this way, you are unreliable in other ways.
- If you cause your spouse to be late with you on a regular basis, your husband or wife will probably feel that you are not only disrespectful of him or her by running late but you are also embarrassing your spouse by causing him or her to be late as well. This syndrome can be a source of great irritation to an otherwise compatible relationship.
- You may have a fear of success, and running late is a form of self-sabotage.

Techniques to break the habit:

- Set all of your clocks to the correct time. The exact correct time. Do not play games with the clock to trick yourself into being on time. You must realize by now that the technique of setting your clocks to the incorrect time does not work.
- Don't plan to be on time anymore; plan on being early. Figure out the actual amount of time it will take you to get to your destination—also factor in time for bathing, dressing, walking to your car, driving, finding parking, and walking to your destination. Now add twenty minutes to the total allowing for unexpected hindrances and so that

you will arrive not on time but early. This extra window of time gets you used to being on time and arriving in a relaxed manner as opposed to a stressed and agitated state.

- Bring a book, a magazine you enjoy, or your laptop to work on so that if being early causes you to have to wait, you will be happy, relaxed, and engaged.

- Use alarms, such as the one in your wristwatch or phone, to alert you when it is time to get ready.

- Motivation: Ask your friends and colleagues (who you consider successful) how they really feel about your being late all the time. Encourage them to be frank with you and not spare your feelings. Listen to them without getting defensive.

- Fill your gas tank at the end of the day on your way home so you never have to stop for gas on your way somewhere. Similarly, stop at an ATM on the day before an event where you may need cash.

- Know your local traffic congestion patterns. Also, when planning your travel, even if it is just a mile away, take into account the weather and other events. Holidays, marathons, etc., could extend your travel time. In some big cities, parking can be very time consuming. When I lived in Los Angeles, I was once late because I had been looking for a parking place for forty-five minutes.

- Keep your wallet and keys in exactly the same place every day at home and at work. Always. That way you can never "misplace" them, creating a last-minute self-sabotaging problem. I knew a man who misplaced his keys almost daily at the office. Whenever he left the office, he spent a stressful five minutes searching for his keys. Of course, he was always running late anyway, so this just made him even more late and more stressed out. Finally, I pointed out that he always knew exactly where he hung his jacket, so why not put his keys in his jacket? I am happy to say he now always knows where to find his keys.

- If you are in an interesting discussion with someone and then you realize it is time for you to go to your next appointment, do not be timid to end the discussion. People understand and will let you go. One thing that makes a more graceful exit is to alert them in advance that you are on your way to a meeting; that way when you announce you need to leave the conversation, they aren't at all surprised. Also, you might say something like, "I need to go to my meeting; is there a time I can call you to continue our talk?" This way you are letting them know that you are sincerely enjoying the discussion so much that you wish to continue it. Remember, if you are polite, it will not harm the relationship, but if you are late, it will most likely tarnish the relationship of the person waiting for you.

- Perhaps you overbook. I knew a CEO who crammed so many meetings in and out of the office that he was late for nearly everything and ended up canceling meetings at the last minute every single day. The result? He irritated every person that he kept waiting and angered every person he abruptly canceled on at the last minute. I knew few who truly respected him.

- Create a consequence that will impact you, an electric fence-type of boundary. Give money to a charity each time you are late. Choose an amount you can barely afford losing so it really hurts if you are late. If you lower the amount so it is insignificant, then the exercise becomes pointless.

CHOOSE YOUR TECHNOLOGY WISELY

Technology is not generally evil in and of itself; in fact, much of it is highly beneficial to humanity. Some of it, however, particularly social technology, can also be a very addictive form of escapism, especially the hand-held or home-entertainment devices. But as futurist and inventor Ray Kurzweil has said, "The power of these technologies and its exponential rise is inexorable, how we apply it is not."[1]

Demand that any technology you bring into your life serves you—not the other way around. Be sure that every device you use, and every way you use it, makes your life simpler, not more complicated. Make sure it gives you more free time, not less of it. Do not be a servant to your technology.

Notice how some devices truly do save you massive amounts of time, like your washing machine. That is a time saver if there ever was one. Before the washing machine, washing clothes was a grueling and extremely time-intensive ordeal. Washing and drying two loads of laundry would have likely taken an entire day of

---

[1] Ray Kurzweil: Get Ready For A Computer In Your Brain – from an interview on Radio Boston March 21, 2011

hard work, plus ironing. Swedish professor and statistician Hans Rosling suggested that the positive impact the washing machine had on the liberation of women makes it "the greatest invention of the industrial revolution."

The trend of appliances marketed in the first half of the twentieth century was mostly as labor-saving devices. Besides the washing machine, other appliances that many of us now take completely for granted, such as the clothes dryer, dishwasher, frost-free refrigerator, food processor, vacuum cleaner, and prepackaged convenience foods, all provide the householder with more free time. But—free time to do what? To spend time with your family and any other interest you may have. It also greatly contributed to women, allowing them time to take a job outside the home and have a career. More recently in the United States and other industrial societies, the majority of devices that are being heavily marketed on television today are not labor-saving devices; they are entertainment/information devices.

Do a short study of the technological devices that you use. For example, your computer may deliver accelerating returns, whereas other devices may ultimately be delivering diminishing returns and mostly just consume your time, like your TV or video games.

Ask yourself the following regarding each new device, software, or app:

1. Does it truly bring more meaning into my life?
2. Is it educationally enhancing or educationally entertaining?
3. Does it enhance the cohesion of my family and community?
4. Will it or does it cause harm to my health by keeping me sedentary too many hours per day?

Next, strategically select which modern conveniences and high-tech devices best serve you and your family. These are all questions that are incumbent upon us now.

Shrink your use of the time-eaters. Remember, your time is your life; it is your life that is being eaten. Every hour you spend in a virtual reality, you lose an hour from actual reality, from your life.

Remember that tomorrow always arrives as today.

Remember that just because it is new, it is not always better. Reawaken your powers of discernment to choose when to har-ness innovation and technology, and when to restore what has served humanity and bound communities together for eons. In my life-time, I can think of dozens of innovations that were clear degrada-tions of what was there before. Like synthetic clothing replacing cotton clothing in the 1970s. There was a huge social backlash to this because we noticed that synthetic fabrics do not feel as good as natural fabrics. Linoleum surfaces do not feel as good as wooden surfaces; imitation chocolate does not taste as good as real choco-late. Fluorescent lighting made us feel bad, whereas natural lighting made us feel good. It is up to us to decide what is an improvement and what we should sustain.Someone once said that the secret to longevity is not how many barrels you have but how full the bar-rels are. Another way of saying it is: To enhance the quality of your years, you must enhance the quality of the days and hours of your life. The things that are often listed as primary causes of happiness are our fam-ily, our spiritual life, our pets, and if we are lucky, our work. On the deathbed people rarely express regret not having spent more time watching reality TV; our regrets are generally personal and spiritual. So, choose how you spend the hours in your life with the greatest care. Money can be replaced, but time cannot.

Suggested ideas for investment of time:

- Invest your time and energy into the three imperatives.
- Invest your time and energy into true friendships.
- Invest your time and energy in ideas and ideals.
- Invest your time and energy into innovation, art, and music.

Some Positive Uses of Technology:

Voice recognition software: Voice dictation is a technology that I now use, and have used it to write parts of this book. For those of you who are like me in that you do not type particularly quickly, we can speak far more words per minute than we can type. Voice dictation is also better for our posture as we can keep our arms down by our sides. So the usual health issues caused from typing, such as tight neck and shoulders and wrist issues, are greatly diminished.

GPS: Personally, I am grateful for my dashboard-mounted GPS in the car. When navigating through a new city without a GPS, it is confusing and dangerous to constantly take your eyes off the road to look at directions or a map, not to mention stress inducing. The GPS is safer, more efficient, and far less stressful. I find that it also helps me to memorize the routes. There is also the option of finding an alternate route when confronted with a traffic jam. If I am in an unfamiliar place and have no idea of what alternate route to take, the GPS is incredibly valuable. In addition, the fact that it can respond to voice commands during driving makes it even one step safer and more practical. With 1.5 million auto-related injuries and about 43,000 auto-related deaths per year in the United States alone, I appreciate technology that highly increases the safety factor on the road.

These are just two simple examples of technological advances that have positively impacted my daily life, and there are countless more. But notice that the two examples include improvement to safety and health and greater efficiency, and both are time savers instead of time stealers.

Poor Uses of Technology:

Text as a principle medium of communication: Observe how many lengthy emails or text messages you write that could be better served with phone calls. When I sit in airports, I often see business people writing long text messages with their thumbs when they could more easily make a phone call. Speaking conveys emotion, and is many times faster than thumb writing and much easier on your overtaxed eyes.

Television as a babysitter: Limited and supervised television viewing can be a mostly positive experience for small children, even educational. But far too often parents rely on television to keep their child in one place, quiet, and occupied. We see the TV to be what people in past generations referred to as "the one-eyed babysitter." The 2012 Nielsen report indicates that children two through eleven years old watch television about three hours and twenty minutes a day. And according to the American Academy of Child and Adolescent Psychiatry, children who watch a lot of television are likely to:

- Have lower grades in school
- Read fewer books
- Exercise less
- Be overweight

The American Academy of Pediatrics recommends discouraging television viewing for children younger than two years altogether and encourages more interactive activities that will promote proper brain development, such as talking, playing, singing, and reading together.

Television as a babysitter is a prime example of poor use of technology because the costs to the child far outweigh the benefits to the child and parent/s.

The self-service kiosk: Replacing friendly employees with self-service kiosks is a trend that, in my view, is shameful. I am sure that the monetary cost-benefit analysis is sound for the bottom line, but the disservice and the cost of good will to the public is evident. We are now asked to interface with a kiosk instead of interact with a friendly and helpful human being, and this continues to isolate us from one another, especially the elderly. For many elderly people, going to a store to buy something might be the only human interaction that they will have that day. To ask a lonely, elderly person to interact with a kiosk instead will just increase the isolation and deep loneliness of so many of our elders. Again, humans need face to face human interaction. We need that ninety percent nonverbal interaction to make us feel sane and whole. Once again, just because it is new does not mean that it is better.

Exercises:

a. Commit to more repose without technology. Learn to sit quietly without the need to touch a button or see if someone somewhere has sent you a text or commented on Facebook. Constant complexity and multitasking is stress inducing. Instead of checking your hand-held device, check in with yourself. For example, if you feel lonely and your first impulse is to go to social media, instead, take a deep breath to redirect your mind and then connect in person with a good friend, or visit someone in your neighborhood. You will get better at this and find that it becomes easier and easier because as your happiness grows, your need for entertainment shrinks. Remember the notorious self-deceptive motto of an addict is, "I can quit anytime I want to, I just don't want to."

b. Establish a personal and unplugged day, a Sabbath of sorts, one day a week with family and friends without the use of electrical devices such as TV, computers, hand-held devices, video games, etc. Get out of virtual reality and into actual reality. Each time you send a text or Facebook message to someone in another location, think about who you are ignoring in your own home. A personal Sabbath will guarantee that your family has at least one day a week together without distraction. It will ensure that you do not forget *how* to be with each other, and although your kids may complain at first, in twenty years I believe that they will look back with great affection for that one day a week when you were all together.

c. What we spend our time on is where we invest our life force. Rethink where you invest your time and energy. Invest more time in friendships and family, into the things that you have identified as things that bring meaning to your life.

d. Develop your highest ideal of life, your life ethos or value system. Or nurture your spiritual life or religion, however you define it, and bring it into everyday living. Take what you learned from the ten questions in the section discussing the first imperative, and begin monitoring your choices to match your priorities. Many people schedule every part of their lives except the most important parts—time to cultivate their deepest beliefs and convictions. Schedule in your one hour of breath-initiated movement every day. Schedule in a gathering at your home with your best friends every month. Schedule in reading time to study topics that make you feel connected to life and inspired to do more with your life span.

e. Stop killing time. Killing time kills you.

THE 10 PERCENT RELATIONSHIP

Our society is currently obsessed with communication via text, especially text messaging. I am constantly amazed that intelligent and kind people still fall into the trap of communicating emotional content via text messaging. This not only falls into the category of stealing your time, but even worse, it is likely harmful to your relationships.

Adding smiley faces :) frown faces :(or symbols of emotions (e.g., LOL) is like trying to create a classic Greek statue with a blunt instrument. Use the right tool for the job. Rule #1: Never communicate about an emotionally charged subject through email or text. If someone sends a negative or emotional email to you, respond with a phone call (not voice mail) or better yet, a sit-down, face-to-face discussion.

For information and simple data, text messaging is a fantastic tool. For example,

Running fifteen minutes late. See you soon.

But text messaging is dreadful for a conversation of an emotional nature, such as,

You embarrassed me at the party. Maybe we should take some time apart.

In fact, for a delicate discussion, text messaging is likely to do more harm than good. You may as well be using smoke signals. This is because text does not convey tone of voice, facial expression, or body posture, so we ultimately guess and superimpose emotions onto the text we read, and very often we are wrong. Consider the above example,

You embarrassed me at the party. Maybe we should take some time apart.

Let's say that Heather wrote this text to her boyfriend, James, an hour after a party. Was Heather, the writer of this text message, terribly sad and crying as she wrote this? Or was she furious and essentially shouting at her boyfriend? James, the receiver of the message has no idea, but he will subconsciously choose whether the text was sad or angry and then respond accordingly. In this scenario, James is in an insecure state, so he will interpret Heather's text as angry and that she wants to break up with him, so even though he loves her, he becomes defensive and texts her back,

OK. You won't be hearing from me again.

In fact, Heather does not want to break up at all, but she believes that James has wanted to break up with her for some time and so has assumed that the incident at the party was a way of communicating this to her. So, Heather is opening the door for him to end the relationship if that is what James truly wants. And interpreted through her fear, James's response confirms this.

Heather, now distraught, quickly shoots back:

Fine.

But James cannot see or hear that Heather is distraught. He receives only her words. And he will continue to assume that she is breaking up with him and is even being nasty about it.

Now, because both of them superimposed the emotion behind the texts through the lens of their fears, both of them believe the other has just ended the relationship, when in fact neither of them truly wants that at all. But if you look at this line of text messages through the lens of their actual feelings, imagining both are devastated, it would look something like this:

> *Heather (crying): You embarrassed me at the party. Maybe we should take some time apart.*
> *James (gutted): OK. (resigned) You won't be hearing from me again. (Tears run down his face.)*
> *Heather (distraught, not knowing what to say): Fine.*

This example is, unfortunately, not far fetched at all. But had this same conversation began in person, James would have seen how sad Heather was rather than angry; he would have realized that she did not want to break up with him in the least bit, and the conversation would have gone an entirely different direction. The bizarre irony in this type of conversation is that both Heather and James are communicating through a device that could also be used as a telephone. They are choosing not to speak to each other but to communicate through text. This is a choice that we must explore and ask ourselves why we would make such a choice. Why would we actively choose to not hear the voice or see the face and eyes of someone with whom we are trying to discuss something delicate and emotional? What are we hiding from?

When a person is in love, to gaze at their beloved's face is heaven itself. No poet will ever write about gazing for hours at her lover's emoticons.

So when it comes to human relations, save text conversations for basic information transfer. To have a discussion that requires the conveyance not only of information but also of emotions, *never use text*. That includes email. Speak face to face in an environment that is conducive to speaking—not somewhere loud and noisy. If it is impossible to speak face to face, then speak on the phone or an Internet service that includes your image in real time, such as Skype or FaceTime. This will give you the other ninety percent of nonverbal information missing from text.

VITAL LIFE: BETTER SLEEP

One-third of our life is spent sleeping, or it used to be anyway. Part of regulating our life is to make sure we set aside adequate time to cultivate restful and nourishing sleep. Since sleeping disorders are now at the level of an epidemic, we must include sleep as part of our work ritual in order to conserve and restore our life-force energy.

When we run out of energy and grow fatigued near the end of the day, our bodies instruct us to rest and repose. But today we are not likely to follow this simple directive. Instead, we may opt for a quick fix via a latte, an energy drink, etc. We drink it, we perk up, we continue working, and we do not ask questions. But from reading the labels, you can see that there is very little energy in energy drinks besides sugar. The caffeine or other stimulants (herbal or not) don't provide us with energy; they trigger our body to release its own stored energy, thereby depleting our bodies even more.

Many people have a good deal of knowledge about their sick hearts, trick knees, or weak stomachs, but in my experience few people discuss what is good for, or harmful to, their nervous system. We speak of the symptoms of a frayed nervous system, such as sleep disorder or depression, but rarely of its care and healing. Stedman's Medical Dictionary describes the nervous system as "the system of cells, tissues, and organs that regulates the body's responses to internal and external stimuli. In vertebrates it consists of the brain, spinal cord, nerves, ganglia, and parts of the receptor and effector organs."

Everyone needs to learn a little bit about energy regulation. Just like your car, even those who know hardly anything about automobiles know that:

a. If you run out of gas, your car will come to a complete stop.
b. If you let the engine oil run out, your car will come to a complete stop—and not ever start again until you replace the engine, and that is very expensive.

Looking at our own human energy systems and the regulation of energy, there are similar concrete rules to live by and a few details to know.

a. Put very simply, we have two batteries: a daily battery and a long-term storage battery. If you drain you daily battery charge, your body needs to rest to recharge that battery. This makes our fatigue later in the evening even deeper and the requirement for sleep more important.
b. If you push forward without rest and consume an energy drink, it will trigger the body to accommodate by switching over to your long-term storage battery and take/steal energy from that source. We are designed to do this on occasion in times of crisis, but not as a lifestyle.
c. If we habitually drain the daily battery through overwork and lack of sleep and instead continually steal energy from our larger battery, then we begin to damage our batteries and energy system. Our digestive system begins to show signs of imbalance, and our immune system weakens. Our nervous system becomes frayed, disrupting our natural

sleep patterns further, and our demeanor more and more resembles someone who has PTSD.

Repose is almost an archaic word in the English language. The definition of *repose* is "a state of rest or tranquility." When a word becomes archaic, it can signify that the meaning or value of the action has degraded from society or even disappeared. For example, we do not use the word *cooper* anymore because the trade of a cooper, a maker or repairer of barrels, no longer exists on a wide scale. *Tranquility* is another word that is becoming archaic. It means "free from disturbance." And to be free from disturbance does not seem to currently be on top of the priority list. The fact that these two words, *repose* and *tranquility*, are disappearing from our language is not surprising because our culture now undervalues rest and tranquility. We value watching TV or playing video games, and we probably believe that these activities are restful because they are entertaining and can divert our minds away from our work or problems, and even make us laugh. But media time, especially violent or stressful games or television shows, is not rest time. It is still fight-or-flight time. Repose triggers the rest and relaxation response, and your mind will know what to do when you tell it that it has some time to rest and rejuvenate. You might just sit with a friend and talk, or sit with a friend and not talk. You might just sit and look at a view or even fall asleep and take an unscheduled nap. Or maybe watch a sunset or sunrise instead of a game show or sporting event. Repose contributes to our calm and tranquility. TV and video games are entertaining, but they still stimulate the brain and cannot count as repose. Schedule repose time into your daily life. Even at work. If people are allowed to step outside for several smoking breaks per day, why can't you step outside the office for five minutes and breathe some fresh air?

What do you do before you go to bed? What has become the new normal is to spend a few hours every evening staring at a big flat screen. Many of us close the day with late-night text messaging or emails or with a last round of social networking. Some even work on the computer right up to the time they shut off the lights. Regardless of the content you are watching on the television monitor, flat screen, computer screen, or smartphone, you are staring at a blue screen.

For the general population in the industrial world, electric lights have only been in existence for about ninety years or less. Prior to electric lights in the home, human beings went to bed shortly after dark as lamp oil and candles were relatively expensive for the average householder. In much of the world, this has not changed even today. For eons, our bodies have been triggered by sunlight and the absence of it to wake up and fall asleep. Our inner clock, known as the circadian rhythm, is an innate schedule of functions, from digestion to brain activity. For sleep, the brain has programmed itself to initiate the secretion of the hormone melatonin at around ten in the evening. Melatonin helps the body to relax into sleep and follow the natural circadian rhythm. However, environmental factors can interfere with the production of melatonin. In our modern electric world, blue light is a major factor. In nature, blue light is part of the light spectrum of sunlight that signals the body to wake up. But now, there are prominent blue-light emitters in our own home: our television screens, computer screens, and smartphone screens all emit blue light. Have you ever noticed that when you drive by a house at night you can see an intense blue light through the window? The people inside the house do not see the blue light; they see a TV program. Outside, where it is dark, the observer sees the light as distinctly blue. So if you spend time staring at a blue screen in the evening, this will likely inhibit melatonin production. Even if you are completely exhausted, due to a lack of melatonin you may not be able to fall asleep. Therefore, to improve your ability to fall asleep and get the rest you need, you should avoid using all blue screens before bed.

Once again, we are taught so little of what is vital for us to know in order to thrive. Getting good sleep and enough of it is arguably more significant to your health than good-quality food. For instance, I met a ninety-two-year-old woman who lived comfortably alone and still drove her own car. She was amazingly lucid, strong, and vital. I decided to find out about her diet, assuming she would have at least one golden nugget to pass along to me. She was a little embarrassed by the question. She admitted that for the last several decades, for her lunch and dinner she had eaten primarily TV dinners (packaged frozen meals). But she had a good night's rest every night.

Do not underestimate the power of sleep. Healthy sleep may be the most underrated health regime that we ignore or abuse at our own peril. Numerous studies cite the benefits of good sleep. Its benefits include improvements in the healing of wounds, concentration, short-term memory, productivity, sensitivity to pain and immune function, digestion, and emotional response to others and life's circumstances. Another detrimental side effect from lack of sleep you will notice is that your muscles tend to contract, and you feel very stiff, especially in the mornings. Then when you get onto your practice mat, you will find stretching ever more difficult due to this contraction. But the most visible side effect from lack of sleep is that we begin to feel tired all day, and when we feel tired all day, we crave high-sugar foods, and this causes us to gain weight.

The issue of good sleep is a difficult one for people in the industrial world because the problem cannot be fixed with a single solution or pill. Imagine if I broke my arm and was taken to an emergency room. Then, after examining me, the doctor tells me that I have a stress fracture and we will need to immobilize it with a cast. The doctor would be quite surprised if I said, *just give me pain pills—forget the cast.* She'd be understandably shocked and would do her best to make me understand the foolishness of suppressing the pain without addressing and treating the injury. That the pain medication will have no impact on healing my arm, and in fact, by numbing the pain without casting the arm, the odds are high that I will make the injury worse. As crazy as this logic of mine sounds, *just give me pain pills,* it is almost exactly what we do with sleep issues (and sometimes pain issues), we go into denial as to the cause and deal only with suppressing the symptoms.

It is important for every person to have some basic understanding of his or her own nervous system, especially in the context of stress. So let's look at it in the context of two states of being: put simply, our nervous system is divided into the sympathetic nervous system (fight or flight) and parasympathetic nervous system (rest and digest). They are not both activated at the same time—one is activated or the other.

The fight-or-flight response (the sympathetic nervous system) is triggered by stress, fear, anger, and grief. When triggered, it speeds up everything that will help you to fight an enemy or run for your life, and it suppresses long-term vital functions like those of the immune system and digestive system. Fight or flight raises your heart rate and blood pressure and releases hormones that will help you in battle while it suppresses digestive activity and the immune system. This is why many people with long-term stress and sleep problems develop digestive problems, such as constipation or diarrhea, and can be more susceptible to colds and the flu as well as outbursts of anger.

When we are not in urgent life-threatening situations, i.e., almost all the time, we are meant to be triggering the rest-and-digest response (the parasympathetic nervous system). It is important to know that the rest-and-digest response does not function when a fight-or-flight response is triggered. For example, every time you consume a caffeine beverage and feel that wonderful surge that revs up your mind and body, you are also simultaneously switching off several important functions, such as the rest-and-digest function of nourishing, healing, and regenerating the body. Rest-and-digest response relaxes the muscles by slowing your heart rate, decreasing your blood pressure, and at the same time increasing the vital digestive and immune system activity. It also acts like an antidote to the stress response. All these get hampered as your morning coffee or energy drink kicks in. If you stay in fight-or-flight mode most of the day, a coveted good night's recovery sleep that you are looking forward to is, to your surprise, not available for you. This is counterintuitive because we feel that in a just universe, when exhausted, our wise and ancient body programming would guide us into perfect sleep so that we can recover from our hard work or dedicated parenting. But alas, this is not so. Because you have spent most of your day triggering your fight-or-flight response, and have done so for years, your nervous system is on alert and will not succumb to the rest-and-digest response easily, and so our sleep is compromised. So, you see, often our sleep issue is a result of our lifestyle during the day. Abuse your nervous system during the day, and your sleep will pay the price. Continue to pay the price at night, and your fatigue will begin to erode your day, and so the vicious circle goes. The solution is obvious. If at all possible, change your day-life to a more balanced and sane routine. The other choice, and unfortunately the more popular one, is what I call "deny-and-suppress," where we choose to ignore all of this and take pills instead.

As previously mentioned, nearly eighty million Americans choose to medicate themselves to sleep. But even here there is a catch with that choice. After taking prescription sleep aids for a year or more, they stop working. Now you need a stronger dose, or a much more powerful medication, and this does not get better; it continues. I have had students approach me at the end of my workshops and privately convey that they are taking the highest dose of the strongest meds legally available to them and are still having problems sleeping and do not know what to do. Humans seem to know no bounds for self-inflicted suffering. I think that it is one of the most astonishing characteristics of our species. On a different occasion, after I had finished lecturing on the benefits of conscious breathing, I mentioned the apparent growing issue of clenching one's jaw during sleep and what is now known by the medical world as TMJD (temporomandibular joint disorder). With this problem, on a minor scale, a person will complain of a sore jaw when first awaking in the morning. It seems that a growing number of people will clench their jaws in their sleep and even grind their teeth during the night so intensely that they wear mouth guards while they sleep. This is because in extreme cases, people will clench their jaws to such extent that they will crack their teeth. One student confided in me that her jaw was so severely clenched shut every morning that the first thing she would do upon rising was to take a hand towel, slide it between her teeth that she can just barely separate, and then pull down on the towel from either side of her mouth to pry her jaw open. This is the most extreme example I have ever heard of. On further discussion, she confessed that she had bottled up a huge wave of anger toward someone and had not been doing anything about it other than the practice of denial and suppression.

From my experiences discussing this with students with a chronic tight jaw, and by observing their emotional state day after day, it seems that the clenching is usually a result of a bottled up rage and/or stress that has been suppressed or repressed.

I must note here that I comment often on the negatives of suppressing your emotions, but there are times in life when it is totally appropriate, such as in times of war, catastrophe, or emergency. During times like these, to dwell on your feelings, to explore and process them, could cause your death or the death of others. When a fight-or-flight response is activated, extra energy is provided to our brain and muscle function, which is just what we need to defeat an enemy or run for our lives. In an emergency, this can be appropriate, in a war it can be appropriate and necessary. But in peacetime, not as a way of life, it is obviously degenerative and hazardous to the survival of the person. When the emergency is over, we must consciously learn to relax again and trigger the switch from fight or flight back to rest and digest. This is the healthy state for the context of a peaceful life.

House cats are fantastic examples of this ability. For example, your cat can be sleeping comfortably when suddenly you burst into the room with an arm full of groceries. In the blink of an eye, your cat is startled awake and jumps in full fighting mode. But then it quickly recognizes you, relaxes, lies down again, and within only a few minutes can be sound asleep once again. You, the human, on the other hand, would react perhaps very differently. If someone bursts into the room and startles you awake so violently that you leap up into battle mode, even though you quickly realize it is only a family member, it is not likely that you will be able to fall asleep for an hour or maybe longer because your body is stuck in fight-or-flight mode. So we need to become more like the cat, able to switch back and forth at will. Far too many of us live in a perpetual fight-or-flight state until our nervous system is frazzled and what used to be peaceful sleep becomes torment.

> "Becoming more relaxed will not disempower you or cause you to be less mentally sharp; conversely, living in a more relaxed state will empower you and help you to not only focus but to also know what is important to focus on."
>
> ~ Max Strom, from *A Life Worth Breathing*

TAKING ACTION: THE BASICS

If you are suffering from sleep problems, put together a comprehensive presleep ritual that you try to adhere to every evening.

Give yourself a twilight time. In nature, the sun dims in intensity as it begins to set, and then we have dusk, which lasts from thirty minutes to one hour. Try ending the day with candlelight and a small reading lamp. Enjoy good conversation, listen to soothing music, or read a book, but be sure to read something inspirational and calming. The body likes routine, so aim to be in bed no later than ten, ready for sleep.

Just before bed, when all other preparations, such as bathing, brushing teeth, etc., are finished, do a short practice that involves four things:

1. Conscious breathing exercises. (Ten minutes)
2. Stretching of the backs of your legs triggers the release of stagnate energy (Qi or Prana) and recalibrates the flow of energy in your body. This simple exercise is known to aid sleep.
3. Seated meditation. Sit on a cushion on the floor, or on a straight-backed chair. (Ten minutes)

4. Legs up the wall. Lie on your back with your legs up the wall. This puts your body in an "L" shape. Your head, back, and sacrum are on the floor. Your buttocks are against the wall, and both legs are vertical, touching the wall. (Ten minutes)

Then get into bed. When you are in bed, you can do slow breathing, elongate your inhaling, and then elongate your exhaling to be twice as long as your inhaling. For example, inhale to the count of four; exhale to the count of eight. This can help further calm you and guide you to sleep.

Give yourself the bare minimum of eight hours before your alarm goes off, longer if you know you need it and have the time to spare. This routine will help your body restore itself to its natural rhythm.

From the first thing you do when you get up in the morning to the last thing you do before you go to sleep at night, do not let your commitment to relaxation falter. Commitment to internal relaxation is a commitment to keeping yourself open, unguarded, and present. Remember, this kind of deep relaxation also fosters deeper intimacy. You become a better listener, and someone with his or her guard down and with an open smile and warm eyes inspires others to be the same.

Lighting

I recommend that in your home and office you consider using light bulbs that are designed to replicate natural sunlight. These bulbs are quite easy to find in home-improvement stores. I find that my body likes this light much more than the yellowish incandescent bulbs or greenish florescent bulbs. In the evening, it is important to dim your lights at least one hour before bed. Candles or oil lamps work best for me as they are natural light sources and feel calming. Using sunlight bulbs during the day and creating a quasi sunset at night can help to support your natural rhythms.

Fresh Air

Air out your house every day, regardless of the season. During the winter, many people do not think of opening their windows for a few minutes to bring fresh air in, and sometimes, extreme weather makes this impossible. But if you can, air out your home every day for just a few minutes. This will add to your health both while you are awake and while you are asleep.

Night Sounds

One fascinating point about our ancient nervous systems is that we are tuned in to the natural sounds of the night in terms of animals and insects. Our nervous system relaxes when we hear crickets chirping or frogs croaking (as long as they are not too loud). Crickets and frogs will not sing when a predator comes near them, and our ancient nervous system seems to know that when the crickets and frogs sing, all is safe—no predators. When they stop singing and everything goes dead silent, a predator is likely very near. So, if dead silence seems to contribute to your insomnia, consider acquiring recordings of these natural sounds to help you sleep. Play the sounds softly.

Not all recordings are done well, so make sure yours has no music on it and the sounds feel relaxing to you. Gentle ocean surf can also be useful, especially if you live in a noisy place, as it will tend to mask unwanted noise. But pay attention to the recording before you purchase. For example, I grew up on the West Coast, so the sound of the Pacific is more soothing to me than the surf of the Atlantic. Even the seagulls' cries sound different. Do not just buy anything that advertises its relaxation benefits. There are a lot of subpar products for sale with very lovely packaging.

Our sense of sound has many purposes. One of them is to keep vigil for warning signs of potential danger. Our brain has not yet adapted to modern house and apartment living, so it is in our self-interest to program sounds that tell our brains that all is safe and soothing.

THE NEW PERSONAL COST-BENEFIT ANALYSIS

A powerful and logical way to help you make healthier decisions is by enhancing a tool already utilized by many every day at work: the cost-benefit analysis.

A normal cost-benefit analysis is, simply put, a process of weighing the total expected costs against the total expected benefits for a business venture or project in order to choose the most profitable option. I have taken this basic form and reworked it into what I call *the new personal cost-benefit analysis*. In this new personal cost-benefit analysis, all benefits and all costs are expressed not only in monetary terms but also in terms of health, impact on family, emotional strain, and your personal definition of happiness and meaning.

During one of my seminars on this subject, a student shared her story of how making a major decision without weighing *all costs* almost, using her words, wrecked her marriage and family. Her husband, who had an above average income, became inspired to purchase his family a wonderful new house that he could just barely afford. To him, this house was a dream come true, and it was clearly important for him to provide such a home for his family. Doing the numbers, he determined that he could *just* afford the mortgage payment for the house if he increased his income by working a few more hours a week. His math was basically sound, but his cost-benefit analysis was incomplete because he was looking at his analysis through *monetary terms alone*. Well, a few more hours a week became working sixty to seventy hours a week, and this caused him (predictably) to not get enough sleep. When he did sleep, it was now a restless sleep, disturbed by stress and worry, which resulted in him grinding his teeth at night. No longer having the time or energy to exercise, he quickly gained weight and grew to be very temperamental as his stress and anxiety levels continued to soar. With his new breakneck schedule, he saw very little of his family, and his children were usually in bed by the time he dragged himself home every night. And when he did see them, he was not good company. His wife told us, "It was killing him, and it was destroying our family. I finally begged him to sell the house and buy something that we can afford. Finally, he relented, and within a short period of time it was like he became ten years younger." Then the woman wiped the tears that were running down her face. The story she relayed to us had clearly been a traumatic period of her life. Her husband was able to work a normal work schedule again and so was now sleeping peacefully, had time for his family, and was in a good mood when he saw them.

In my view, it is clear that what her husband did not calculate into his analysis was this:

Costs:	Benefits:
Happiness	
Family time	
Sleep/Rest	
Exercise	
Ethics	
Overall Health	

Exercise:

Do a personal cost-benefit analysis of what you do now with regard to your job, your home, etc., and adjust your life according to the results you discover. If you begin a new business or job that will greatly increase your monetary income but will require that you work seventy-hour weeks for a few years, what will be the cost to your health? To your family? Because if you lose either you will lose everything. Your family will see much less of you. And when they do see you, will you be too fatigued to enjoy each other? Even though you may make a lot of money from this venture, will you hate doing it, and will that cause you to be a volcano of frustration and, therefore, difficult to be around?

If you become too obsessed with working, you will lose your health or your family, and then you lose everything. Can you afford that?

Those of you out there working sixty-hour weeks to put your kids into the best schools may be making a mistake. Your children need you at home and present more than they need to go to the best schools. Your time with your children is priceless. They will forgive you for not being able to afford the best schools, or even for their having to pay for their own education, but they may not forgive you for being an absent or neglectful parent. The purpose of your life on earth is not to put your kids into the best schools so that they can put their kids into the best schools and so that they can put their kids into the best schools.

Now the argument that might pop up in your mind is, "Couldn't I do more for humanity if I were very wealthy?" My answer is, look for examples. Make a list of the most spiritually influential people in the last one thousand years and then look at their state of materialism. The answer will be self-evident.

Suggestions to decrease stress:

- Decrease noise in your life. In general, see if you can become more sensitive to sound in your work and home. Just like removing clutter from your environment, decrease unnecessary noise from your life as noise has a negative and tensing effect on your nervous system.
- Invest some of your new free time to the third imperative. Practice a daily regime such as yoga or qigong.
- Simplify obligations. Start booking free time as a significant event.
- Experience more of your life span in nature. The more time we spend in nature, the more we feel human, whole, and alive.

ASHES IN YOUR EYES

In nearly every person's life, a total reassessment of priorities is triggered from time to time. This is usually caused by extraordinary, cathartic epiphanies, whether from tragic or joyous events, that open our eyes to our inner world and we are cracked open. What is revealed is a momentary glimpse at the essence of who we really are. This can spark spontaneous and sudden growth at the innermost level, altering the course of our life. Emotional transformation shapes our intellectual understanding of our world because it provides context, so an emotional epiphany or a sudden insight into the essential meaning of life can cause powerful changes of direction. The road of our life is marked by such events. At these times, it is as if we look down at a village from a hilltop. From there we can see our life as if for the first time and we begin to connect the dots that link our life together. We may begin to see that we have devoted too much time on things that have almost no lasting impact while learning little of things that are vital to our well-being or health. For example, many people know more details about their favorite celebrities or sports heroes than about their closest friends. We also begin to notice that much of our society's perception of the word is . . . inaccurate.

One of the events in my own path that contributed to my being jolted awake long enough to change the trajectory of my life occurred in India almost fifteen years ago. My traveling companion and I arrived by train into the teeming city of Varanasi, having just recovered (mostly) from traveler's sickness.

Varanasi is considered by Hindus as one of the holiest cities and is a destination of pilgrimage for Hindus of all denominations. Hindus believe that bathing in the water of the Ganges river remits sins and that dying in Varanasi ensures release of a person's soul from the cycle of death and rebirth. Many Hindus travel to the city specifically to die, be cremated on the ghats, and have their remains placed into the river.

It is likely that you have seen beautiful photographs from India of people bathing as a spiritual ritual on the ghats of the Ganges River; these photos are usually from Varanasi. A ghat is a series of steps leading down to a body of water, usually a holy river or lake. You may also have seen some photographs, although rare, of the outdoor burning funeral pyres on the Manikarnika Ghat, which is the primary site for Hindu cremation in the city.

On our first sojourn down the ghats, we found ourselves near some sort of indistinguishable gathering on the ancient stone steps. Upon seeing the billowing smoke, we discovered that we had inadvertently arrived at the burning ghats. We were taken aback at the sight of seven bodies wrapped in muslin cloth that were just set ablaze. The families in mourning sat just above the pyres, just out of reach of the flames. The widows were dressed in white robes and had shaved their heads. My friend and I looked on for just a moment and then thought we should move away from them, as we felt like intruders disturbing something very personal and sacred. As we turned to leave, one of the attendants in charge of the burning approached us and asked us to stay. He ignored our discomfort and objections and, instead, led us through the crowd and gestured for us to sit on the steps only forty feet away from the burning corpses. He left us to observe the sacred event after pointedly delivering the phrase "cremation is education." It was an axiom instantly memorized, especially in those circumstances. We both sat in silent contemplation with the afternoon sun glaring through the thick smoke. I watched the attendants stoke the fire with long poles and even push and break off the charred limbs from the bodies. It was my first time seeing bodies burning on a pyre, and it is just not the same as seeing it in a documentary or in photos. Not at all. As the muslin cloth wrapping burned away, I could see the feet and hands of the bodies turn black and was moved by the weeping of the grieving families nearby. After a time, I decided to use this extraordinary opportunity to engage in a form of active mediation I had read about many years earlier, a practice to help one realize the impermanence of the body. The concept is that when a person truly understands how short his or her mortal life is, he or she will be launched into a deeper state of reality and live a profoundly richer life. The practice is simple: What you do is imagine that the corpses you are watching are the bodies of your loved ones, the people that you love the most in the world. In other words, you make it as personal as possible.

After focusing my imagination on this for a while, the vision became very real. With open eyes brimming with tears, I saw seven of the most beloved people in my life burn in the flames. It was profoundly moving, and I found myself grieving deeply. The next step of the practice is to imagine that one of the corpses is your own body. I selected one of the bodies closest to me and, in my mind, converted the identity to that of my own flesh and bone and watched the flames envelop and consume it. Just as this happened, a gust of wind whipped toward us, blowing smoke and ash our way. As I watched my own body burn, the ashes from the pyre blew into my eyes and covered my face and hair as if punctuating the reality of what was happening. I don't know how long we sat there—perhaps two hours—but I do know that on our walk back up the ghats in the light of the sunset, covered in the ash of the dead, I knew that I was going to make some changes in my life because my mortal life was running out; even if I were to live another hundred years, my body will one day be ash on someone else's face. I knew that there was more to do, that I was being held accountable by something deep within me, and that something told me that I had better get busy.

If you desire to accelerate your growth, you can't wait for life to randomly present you with extreme situations or circumstances that will jolt you awake. To choose to transform, heal, and grow is the dynamic and noble path that so few take but all of us admire. And the path of personal transformation is open to any person who chooses it, regardless of social or economic class, age, or race.

To increase the depth of life in each day, in each moment, following a daily practice using the three imperatives can keep you in a more awake, aware, and present state. From this clearer state you can then intentionally step outside your box, as they say, the box of your social framework, and see things as they are rather than how you were taught or how you assume they are.

> Social framework in this case refers to the customs, ideologies, and beliefs absorbed through family life, religion, school, entertainment, and popular culture.
>
> Each day, look at your life with new eyes and reassess what is truly of value and what is not, what to dispense with and what to nurture, and perhaps most of all, into what you should invest your most precious resource—your time. In this way you begin to connect the dots that connect your life together.
>
> *When you die, the only thing that you will take with you is three yards of white cloth—the cloth that they wrap your body in.*

**IMPERATIVE 3:
LEARN AND PRACTICE A DAILY
REGIME THAT HEALS, EMPOWERS,
AND ILLUMINATES**

The Imperative of Transformation

What are some of the things we do every day that contribute to stress? To begin with, far too many of us work too many hours in a day. The second most obvious, common, and controllable culprit in my opinion is overdosing on caffeine. Caffeine in moderation is fine, but if we are grinding our jaw at night or if we blow up in anger at people, or if we're irritable much of the time, then we might want to think about cutting back on our intake. Television is another culprit. Although we like to watch TV at the end of the day to relax, I have observed that people who watch a lot of TV are usually not relaxed at all. And then there's the computer. Imagine yourself sitting there at your computer all day with poor posture and five diet sodas or several lattes surging through your bloodstream. What's your breathing going to be like? Later, when you are driving home, your overly fatigued eyes have to deal with objects flying by you at sixty-five miles an hour. Then you suddenly have to brake for a hellish traffic jam, and now you are stopped completely—trapped. And of course you have the news on the radio blaring its daily stream of negativity. We live like this, *electively*, in what is essentially a stress-based life, and then we wonder why we are not feeling well.

The stress of our day-to-day lives keeps us in an almost constant state of fight-or-flight tension, and over the years, to our detriment, we become habituated and the tension builds and builds. What do we call this imbalanced state? We now call it normal. This new "normal" at some point requires us to start taking a pill or two. High blood pressure medication, antidepressants, antianxiety drugs, and/

or sleeping pills are what we turn to in order to cope. We do not heal anything with these pills; we just cover up the imbalance and carry on with the same behavior. If we accept that we are going to live in long-term anxiety, we are also accepting that we will often emotionally overreact or underreact to challenging situations. In other words, we will overreact in a fight response or underreact in an emotional withdrawal response. We urgently need to get out of the fight-or-flight state and live once again with a relaxed nervous system. Without a daily regime that heals, opens, and empowers you, your body will plague you with desires and cravings and with the ruinous results of those cravings—eating disorders, alcohol, cigarettes, sugar, caffeine, etc., and then insomnia, headaches, flu, restlessness, and depression. There is no escape. If you truly desire to rise to a new level, to transform, you must first heal, empower, and liberate your body. This can have an enormous impact on your health, your ability to sleep through the night, your relationships, and even your life span.

A NEW KIND OF FITNESS: HEALING THE SPIRIT

Before we talk about movement, breathing, or the mind, let's start at the very beginning. Within each of us, there is luminosity, the light of conscious awareness, or spirit. It manifests as the voice of the intuition that guides us along our path through life. It is the light that shines from the eyes of a healthy and vibrant person. The healthier the spirit, or the more uncovered the spirit, the more a person will be living the life he or she was meant to live. But a person's spirit can be disturbed or even shattered. When the spirit is disturbed or traumatized, our human energy system becomes disharmonious and manifests symptoms such as:

Hyperactivity and restlessness
Anxiety
Insomnia
Poor concentration
Self-doubt
Chronic fatigue
Depression

As a teacher, I see people on a regular basis who have symptoms of PTSD but who have never been near a battlefield; they are simply veterans of an overly stressful or traumatic life. In our New Cambrian Age, the spirit is commonly strained to its very limits by overwork and prolonged anxiety. It can also be triggered by sudden and intense grief or trauma from heart-break, abuse, or war. Constant absorption into the world of blue screens seems to also have its role in this negative impact, and of course, substance abuse can also severely damage the spirit. But the gifts from nourishing and healing the spirit are many. From my personal experience and from observing the healing process of countless students, the benefits of healing the spirit can be clearly seen by the emergence of these healthy indicators:

Your sleep improves.
Depression lifts.
Your insight and intuition return.
Anxiety dissolves into a sense of trusting yourself.
You begin to crave integrity and kindness in your relationships.
You begin to once again make choices that cultivate an authentic life path.

It is clear to me that sometimes for the body to heal, we must heal a disturbed spirit. A renowned acupuncturist once told me that, in her opinion, ninety percent of her patients needed a long vacation more than any other treatment.

Society teaches us very little about the nature of happiness and dealing with negative emotions. One of the most important and invaluable tools for healing our spirit and enhancing our emotional health is to make sure that negative emotions do not accumulate and become congested. One of the primary things to understand is that our emotions are expressed, felt, and stored in our bodies. Everyone can feel when there is tension in the room. When we get angry, our faces look angry, and our bodies vividly express anger as we clench our fists, tense our jaws, or start to frown. When we feel grief, we start to cry, a physical expression, tears run down our faces, and we slump over as our lungs begin to spasm. It's a physical experience to feel emotions, and people around us can see and feel our emotions because our bodies clearly express them.

There is a mistaken assumption that when the wave of anger or grief subsides, it is entirely gone and we are clean slates again. What seems to really happen is that when we experience intense negative emotions long enough and often enough, we accumulate these negative emotions over the years and store them in our bodies. This negative energy will build with tension and eventually begin to sabotage our own happiness and health.

Some say we store our emotions in the cells of our body, some say in our fasciae, some say in our organs, some say in our brain. It does not really matter; what does matter is that we recognize that more than memories can be triggered by an experience, and the trauma—the actual physical trauma—can be relived again. Some skeptics balk at the idea that we store emotions in the body, yet if you think about it, there are examples of this all around you every day—right now. For example, your boss may come into the office in an obviously bad mood. She had an argument with her husband over breakfast, and now by the way she walks across the room, everyone in the office can tell she is visibly irritated. It is obvious because her body is expressing it—her walk, sharp movements, erratic breath, and of course, her glare. At the end of the day, it is even worse. The stress of her workday accumulates in her body, provoking her disturbed spirit and accentuating her already angry state; and now everyone avoids even making eye contact with her for fear of a confrontation. This is an example of accumulated and stored negative emotions. This syndrome of stored emotions is reflected in the ancient analogy, "The straw that broke the camel's back."

Another example: If you study the faces of the elderly, quite often you can see a lifetime of negative emotions permanently etched in their faces as anger lines, or a constant expression of disappointment, etc. We probably all have known an angry old man or woman who seems to wake up resentful in the morning and goes to bed with a scowl.

Yet another example: Military veterans retuning home with PTSD are very lucid examples of human beings carrying stored emotions in their bodies. After soldiers with PTSD remove their uniforms and return to the comfort and safety of their homes, they can frequently reexperience the original trauma, or traumas, from war through flashbacks and nightmares. During the day, loud noises or sudden movements can cause them to spring into emergency-level action as if they are in full battle, and they can fall into seemingly out-of-the-blue episodes of grief.

After careful and common sense observation of human beings, it is clear that:

- We experience our emotions in our body.
- We express emotions with our body, including and especially our face.
- Our emotions are often stored in our body for long periods, even for decades.
- Suppressed or repressed emotions can be released from the body through high-level bodywork, hatha yoga, some exercises, and finally and especially breathwork.
- A daily regime of conscious breathing helps to manage and purge emotional pain and stress.
- Our mind, our body, and our emotions are not really separate. Each one affects the others.

What we need is a daily health regime for the rest of our life. Choose a movement exercise regime that not only changes the body but also cleanses it of accumulated negative emotions and harmonizes the nervous system. The two regimes that already possess the majority of techniques that you will need to heal your spirit are hatha yoga and qigong.

CONSCIOUS BREATHING

Is it possible that our health issues, stress issues, and spiritual issues are all related to our breath? I am convinced that they are, which is why I teach conscious-breathing workshops in about forty-five cities and ten countries every year. I have seen tens of thousands of people respond to breathwork in extraordinary ways, and I am privileged to witness this every week. I teach people to look into their bodies and then to move their bodies by initiating movement with steady breathing. We are breathing right now, but we are not breathing in a transformative way; we are breathing in an autopilot way, just enough to survive.

Breath-initiated movement is what could be called the prime mover. Our breath accesses universal energy called Prana, or Qi, and this energy, when invited into our system, revitalizes our energy, our life, and our strength. Breath-initiated movement can spark the higher nature that is within us, which seeks the creation of happiness in our lives. When we breathe in a certain way, every day, there is a cumulative effect, which helps to keep our nervous system calm. If we do not keep our nervous system calm, we are probably at some point going to end up having to medicate ourselves. Sometimes people do not connect these dots and continue to wonder why it is so important to calm their nervous system as they wash down their daily blood pressure medications or antidepressants. You might wonder what breathing has to do with our emotions. After all, isn't breathing simply a physical function dealing with the exchange of oxygen and carbon dioxide? Aren't emotions just feelings? But then you should also ask what a pint of ice cream has to do with managing loneliness. Or, why is it that a thirty-minute foot rub can convert a scientist with an IQ of 160 into a happy drooling three-year-old? Why does stubbing your toe cause you to become enraged and cursing with anger? And why do human beings, when struck with grief, experience lung spasms? There is obviously more to our emotions and our breath than many of us have been assuming all these years.

Remember, earlier in the book I mentioned that the only people who are taught how to breathe on a wide scale are pregnant women. Modern medicine seems to have acknowledged that breathing techniques help manage fear and pain, increase focus, calm the body, and decrease physical distress, but apparently only for women giving birth. The expecting mothers are taught that their new breathing practice is only for giving birth and for nothing else. Aside from childbirth, every single person is faced with the same challenges in life, more or less. We all experience fear, anger, physical pain, and certainly plenty of stress. We all find ourselves at some point desperately needing to focus amidst a chaotic situation. Then is it not logical for us all to learn how to breathe as an important life skill—not only as a skill to turn to in crisis or extreme circumstances but also as a daily practice of sustaining and recalibrating our nervous system?

Breathing requires no incense, candles, statues, or a guru. It is yours to use when you need it and to prepare for any challenging situation, including dense traffic or even discreetly while in a business meeting. It is clear that when we practice a daily regime of breath-initiated movement, we are not just working out, we begin to heal our entire life; we open the door to a new life. This is a system for accelerating our personal evolution. It is where we begin to put transformational concepts into action and thereby set into motion transformation in the world. Learn to cultivate your best intention, grace, and awareness as you breathe and move. This will not only elevate your experience to a higher level, it will change how you are perceived by others.

YOUR EMOTIONAL BODY

Remember that ninety percent of human communication is non-verbal and that a vast amount of our emotions and thoughts are expressed and experienced in our bodies. Much of the time, our body language is protective, even somewhat fearful and rigid. Just sit in a public place and watch people walking by with this in mind. We become so accustomed to protecting ourselves that we forget we are even doing it; in fact, most of the time we are on guard even when there is no danger; even while alone in a room, our body posture is still on guard—our shields still up.

Think of your body as the physical part of your mind and emotions. It is your mind and emotions, in essence, that create your body. For example, your posture, whether it is strong and upright or slouched with a concave chest, is mostly directed and sustained by how you feel. One way to heal your emotions is to manipulate the body in a positive way. Simply by lying in certain restorative postures every evening at home will help begin the process. It will help you learn to breathe; it will help you open the chest and shoulder area. When you do this, you will feel a release of stress, worry, and anger. The end result is that you feel much better and, not surprisingly, kinder. You see, you can't have your guard up and be kind at the same time. It does not really work because the intentions are in opposition. Imagine a crab sitting under a rock with its claws sticking out in a battle-ready stance—it is a powerful protective position, and it works well as a defense from aggressors, but it is hard to make friends from that position because all that people see is your claws.

It is my deepest belief that your exercise regime should be a living part of your spiritual life or ideal of life, manifesting who you are in the world with your living body as your medium. Achieving health, happiness, and meaning through a daily healing practice is ever more crucial as we eventually increase our life span up to 100–150 years. Breathing practices, meditation, and conscious movement are all essential.

The third imperative encompasses the principles that integrate and harmonize the mind, emotions, and body. The guidelines and core principles that I present here should integrate naturally with nearly all religious paths and philosophies. The primary intent of the third imperative is to guide you to embody your own ideal of life or religion and to learn to breathe what I call the ultimate source of life. This source I refer to is that which is beyond what our intellect can grasp but what the heart knows intimately. To name it and put a face on it drives men insane—insane to the point of going to war to ensure that their name/s of the unnamable and their stories of the indescribable are imposed by the point of a sword, the bullet of an AK-47, or the shrapnel of an IED (improvised explosive device). We must not forget that words, names, and terms are only symbols, and symbols are not the objects themselves. Words are pitifully limited; for example, we can barely describe our feelings of romantic love, so we leave such word artistry to the poets and songwriters. To use these same limited symbols to describe that which is beyond describing is a fool's task, like counting grains of sand on the beach instead of appreciating the golden sunrise on the horizon. Artists, musicians, and dancers discovered long ago that some indescribable phenomenon can be expressed better in mediums other than words and often far more successfully. I have listened to many pieces of music that in my experience portray a glimpse of the source much more powerfully than any scribbled words. So let us portray, express, and communicate our spirituality in our breath and movement. Some Taoists beautifully describe the graceful Chinese practice of qigong as a person acting as a conduit between heaven and earth. The third imperative is not an attempt to expound one particular style of yoga or qigong or any other ritualized regime but instead to elucidate essential and practical principles and techniques that can be integrated and applied to whatever movement or yoga routine you use now, or to help you select a more empowering regime based on these core principles. Whenever we take the right action in life, there are always far-reaching benefits besides the obvious one at hand.

INHABITING THE BODY

If you want to be happy, relax more, and sleep better, you must be honest with yourself and ask yourself if you are achieving your goals. If not, it is time to take a proactive approach to your health and happiness rather than a reactive and suppressive one. Most of us have grown up with a false illusion of fitness. Most of us believe that exercising a few times a week by engaging in a casual sport, such as tennis, jogging, bicycling, or lifting weights, will be enough to keep us fit for the rest of our lives.

Many of us, overwhelmed by life, cease exercising for a number of years, and then when we finally decide to start again, we go back to exercise techniques that we learned in high school, techniques long ago discarded in the athletic world as unsafe. The only reason those techniques did not hurt us before is that we were young and resilient. But after we have passed the age of thirty, and we cannot abuse our bodies by making the same demands on it that we did in our twenties.

Some of us commit to more strenuous fitness regimes, such as various aerobic routines, and more recently we have seen the emergence of new and ultra dynamic fitness regimes, often with extreme titles to imply military or Olympian level of physical transformation that promises six-pack abs in just a few months and a body to be proud of when you look into the mirror.

Let's consider these briefly from a different perspective: Some sports, such as tennis and basketball, are truly fun and engaging. They are aerobic and have many other benefits, such as toning the body while also challenging the mind. They improve hand-eye coordination and reflexes. But they are also well known for repetitive stress and motion injuries, particularly to the knees, elbows, shoulders, and lower back.

Bicycling, which I myself enjoy, has many benefits, but the range of motion of the legs is extremely limited and mostly unchanging for the average cyclist. It strengthens only the lower body muscles in a very incomplete way. The aerobic benefits are obviously significant, but without meaningful stretching afterward, lower back problems will emerge. The arched back position of most cyclists can not only contribute to lower back issues but it also draws the ribcage in, causing physical restriction of the chest that enables only shallow breathing.

Jogging is an incomplete, yet partly beneficial, workout if the runner has a healthy gait and runs on soft and uneven surfaces rather than on flat, hard surfaces. Yet most joggers that I have observed do not do either. They do not study how to move their bodies in a healthy alignment and usually also run on hard pavement or asphalt, so runners often fall victim to repetitive stress injuries or repetitive motion injuries while neglecting upper body exercise. High-tech running shoes will not compensate for poor gait or damage done by running on cement or asphalt, no matter how much they cost.

As I work with a great deal of people over fifty years old, I am constantly meeting people who have had, or will soon have, knee or hip replacement surgery due to a few decades of these types of exercises.

Those who run on a treadmill or similar fitness machines bypass some of these common injuries, but so many now run while distracting themselves with a screen in front of them. This is understandable behavior especially with something as unchanging as running in a straight line on a conveyor belt. In days gone by, this kind of exercise was reserved only for pet rodents in cages, the classic hamster wheel, but now we humans have adopted it for ourselves as well. This kind of exercise is understandable and sometimes necessary, particularly if you live in a place where there are no good/safe trails to run on or if the weather is too inclement to step outdoors. In my travels, I sometimes use (reluctantly) these machines myself. They get my heart beating and my blood surging, but I find them almost dehumanizing. Nearly all the hotels equip their stationary machines with small flat screens mounted on the handlebars to allow us to disassociate from the drudgery at hand and to lose ourselves to something entertaining. But I believe this creates its own kind of damage that I call repetitive disassociation syndrome. We learn to abandon our mind to a TV show or movie while simultaneously switching off body awareness beyond the essential signals needed to keep the repetitive movement on track. Intentional disassociation from our body can be a dangerous habit. I believe that to have the body run mindlessly like a robot while the mind concentrates on a virtual reality creates its own new set of problems. While you are, on the one hand, exercising your body every day, you are also teaching your mind to disassociate from your body every day and reinforcing this habit of separating, rather than unifying, movement, breathing, and concentration. This trains you to not feel what your body is feeling, which is another way of saying that you are committed to a daily regime of numbing your body.

When you think about it, it is obvious how this happens. It would be like making love with someone while watching a TV show across the room—not ideal for any kind of intimacy or connection, not to mention loving respectful behavior. You may be thinking, *If running on a treadmill were more like making love, I wouldn't need the TV.* The treadmill is boring. I contend that whatever exercise you choose, it is in your great interest to keep your awareness in your breath and movement, even in monotonous circumstances. I urge you to, as a rule, not make monotonous exercises part of your daily regime. One of the pleasures of yoga, qigong, and tai chi is that the movements and postures are not monotonous; there is a variety of movements and challenges requiring the mind to constantly adapt and calibrate. This is not only direct association of the mind, breath, and body, it is far beyond that; it is an ever-enhancing relationship.

Imagine a horse wearing blinders and pulling a carriage though city streets, clopping down the same route over and over, day after day. Now imagine a wild horse running freely through mountainous trails, completely engaged and present, fully attuned to his surroundings, and you can see a primitive illustration of what I mean. The horses in the city often look sad, their spirits tragically broken. But I have had the chance of looking into the eyes of a wild stallion when we happened upon each other in the Nevada wilderness some forty years ago. We stared at each other from only a few yards away for an infinite few seconds, and I can tell you that his spirit was one of the most magnificent I have ever seen. Although I was full-grown, I felt like a small child in his magnificent presence. If you teach yourself to disassociate from your own body, you may be contributing to the breaking of your own spirit, and you may automatically and unconsciously use your power of disassociation whenever you feel threatened or overwhelmed, as there is now a pattern of defensive dissociation. Like the metaphor of the basket of light, the basket/armor keeps away everyone, not just enemies, and the dissociation from your body is similarly undiscriminating. This work has low impact on the knees and high impact on your life.

Over a decade ago, a woman of about thirty years old began practicing in my hatha yoga class. She was, on first observation, a healthy and vibrant person. But as I studied her expression while she practiced, I perceived what I believed to be the expression of physical pain on her face. At some point I approached her and quietly asked her if she was in pain. She emphatically said, "No." I was puzzled to learn that my perception had given me false signals, as it was generally very dependable. Later I watched the young woman's face again, and I read the same signals—she was repressing physical pain. After class, I took her aside and told her that her face showed signs of physical pain, but she kindly assured me that I was mistaken and that she was fine. The next time I saw her was several weeks later. She had a bandana on her head, and her face looked swollen. She took me aside and told me that shortly after her last class with me, she went to the doctor for what she believed was an ulcer and that despite her trying to convince me otherwise, she was experiencing some stomach pain. What the doctor discovered was that her abdomen was riddled with tumors, and she was given a prognosis of stage IV cancer. The bandana on her head was to cover her baldness due to the chemotherapy treatment she was now undergoing. To me, this was a case of disassociation syndrome. This young woman had learned not to listen to her body and, therefore, could not sense that something had gone very wrong within. Fortunately, somewhere within her medical treatment and what was now her daily breath-initiated yoga practice, she experienced what some call a miracle and survived the cancer. It went into full remission, and as of the publishing of this book, she has been cancer free for thirteen years. When we spoke of this recently, she expressly added that yoga helped her to tune into the part of her that wasn't physical, and she strongly believes that this was of huge importance in her healing.

In another case, many years ago I worked with a professional football player who said to me something to the affect of, "Max, I need you to teach me how to sense what my body is telling me, because I do not know how to tell if I am feeling pain anymore." This man, who was a fierce warrior on the football field, had pushed on through physical pain and injuries so often and to such an extreme that he virtually blocked sensation from his body. Thankfully, after practicing a breathing regime, he realized to what level he had shut down and now earnestly wished to heal and reconnect.

WHY STRETCHING?

One of the greatest roadblocks to get around in the fitness mindset is that stretching is a waste of time. Stretching is a critical missing piece in everyday sports, both within the sport itself and at the end of the routine. Many weight lifters practically ignore stretching as a relevant practice. I think the reason is that most of us would rather not exercise, and the one thing that motivates us to do so is the desire to look more attractive to others by losing weight and/or enhancing the shape of our bodies. As a result, we tend to gravitate toward exercises that are contraction-based (muscle building) rather than stretching-based. This is because, as we all know, contraction-based movement enlarges, tones, and firms muscles. Weightlifting is the most obvious example of this. In weightlifting, you do repetitive contraction movements that develop and shape your muscles, but there is little emphasis on sufficiently stretching the muscles afterward, if at all. Joggers are also notorious for not stretching enough after a run. I have sat on a park bench and watched multiple joggers complete their runs and proceed to stretch their legs for a grand total of ninety seconds. One-hour jogging followed by ninety seconds of stretching. *Ninety seconds!* Burning calories and strengthening muscles as the central theme of exercise is, in my view, an archaic paradigm. They are important pieces but only fragments of a complete practice. Stretching elongates muscles and, contrary to some mythology, is not counterproductive to getting in shape or "only for girls." While women will often not invest much effort into stretching because they are "not losing weight," men often disregard it altogether as a total waste of time.

Stretching regularly with healthy technique will relax the muscles, which begins triggering the rest-and-digest response, which can, in turn, help you to digest food properly and to sleep. Stretching regularly also increases your overall flexibility and range of motion. Although this is often emphasized as a benefit for high-level athletes to enhance performance and reduce the risk of injury, I think it is more relevant that it is health enhancing in these same ways for both women and men. Stretching incorporated with strength building exercises also leads to improved balance, coordination, and greater body awareness. After all, to stretch, you must focus on the sensations you are feeling so that you apply enough effort to stretch the muscles but not as much as to risk tearing them.

This is a basic biofeedback mechanism that has broader benefits. For example, if you learn to listen for your baby crying from its crib, you are training yourself to listen for your baby—period. You will notice all sounds from the bedroom and your baby, not only crying. Similarly, if you learn to listen to your body in terms of what it needs while stretching, I think you become a better listener to your body regarding all sensations and warning signs.

Every cat and dog stretches many times throughout the day. It is a fantastic instinct that they follow after waking from a nap or after long periods of inactivity. We humans have the same basic instinct, and if well rested, we will stretch and yawn in the mornings. But stretching only a few times a day for three or four seconds at a time is not transformational or nearly enough for the chair-bound species we have become.

Hatha yoga incorporates a considerable amount of stretching, but many have the misconception that yoga is only a stretching class for already flexible people, nothing more, and that a yoga teacher is just a stretch coach in tights. This is an unfortunate stereotype that prevents many from signing up for their first class. In fact, hatha yoga, if taught by an adept teacher, involves strength building as well as the stretching of the major muscle groups. Besides strength building and stretching, balance and reflexes are also developed as well as focusing and calming the mind. Long-time yoga practitioners are well known for accessing postures unattainable to the novice, and an undereducated teacher may emphasize the striving toward more and more complicated or challenging postures; in my opinion, however, this is a misunderstanding of the purpose of hatha yoga by the teacher.

I believe that human beings were not created to force themselves into yoga postures; yoga postures were created to heal human beings. The postures are our tools, not our goals. We choose postures that best serve us in our current state of health and in the healing of our injuries. If someone is locked up and tight everywhere, there will be an emphasis on stretching. But if a novice student is hyperflexible and weak, the emphasis should not be on stretching but on strengthening and stabilizing. For an individual with a hyperactive nature, the emphasis of his or her practice should be centering and calming work, and to one who is more lethargic, the focus should be on postures and movement to stimulate and energize the student.

To be flexible and fluid is important. But to have a container, or structure, is also important. The container holds the fluid and gives it form. When you have both the container and fluidity, then what you have is the Holy Grail.

Stretching can also be dangerous when enacted without guidance and with force. From my experience as a teacher, most people tend to force themselves deeper into postures because they are still in the competitive mindset, so I spend a lot of time urging students to go easy and take their time. I use the metaphor of a volume knob on an mp3 player. Zero means you feel nothing; ten means you are tearing your muscle. You must learn to feel one through eight and practice at about four or five. If you think you are possibly overdoing it, assume that you are, then back off. Tearing a hamstring or groin muscle (for example) can take one to two years to heal. It is an awful experience. So, as your stretch, when you find yourself clenching your teeth, you are pushing too much. If you cannot breath deeply in and out of the chest, you are overstretching. I repeat these types of warnings again and again during the movement part of my classes to retrain the student's mind to use other tools besides force and power. I believe that it is critical to educate the students to associate and listen to their bodies so that their practice is a transformative one that will yield untold benefits, and not a new sport to push their way through, tearing muscles and causing permanent damage to the tendons and ligaments.

Just like breath-initiated movement, stretching should also be led by your ocean breathing. It can become breath-initiated stretching. I teach the technique of slightly decreasing the stretch while you inhale and then moving slightly deeper into the stretch as you exhale. When your breath is the master of your stretching, your sensitivity to your body increases. It can feel like your body listens to your breath as your breath guides it.

As a general rule, I recommend equal time spent in strength building and stretching. Runners or cyclists who train for an hour should commit to a minimum of thirty minutes of stretching afterward with conscious breathing, and the result will be body consciousness you did not know was available to you.

CUTTING-EDGE FITNESS REGIMES

Some of the new, more sophisticated hybrid fitness regimes that are becoming more common now have a fantastic balance of strength building, aerobic exercise, and stretching. I will say that at the top of the pyramid of exercise routines, stretching seems to be becoming increasingly significant, but it has yet to reach the average person in the gym.

Sometimes I present my work at large conferences that are primarily cutting-edge fitness-centric, and I think that many of the workouts that are taught at these conferences are now very sophisticated and well thought-out. Many of the conference attendees come to my workshops and seminars to try something new. In these conference environments, I am exposed to hundreds of people who are (what would be commonly categorized as) quite physically fit. They are strong, they stretch, and they are aerobically fit, but on observing the state of their nervous systems—their inner lives, so to speak—the majority of the students that I witness at these conferences are obviously under great stress. They do not appear inwardly calm or happy, and many have very restless spirits. Some are clearly addicted to working out and suffer from constant hunger from their extreme calorie restrictions. Again, I must emphasize that some of the fitness regimes are very well designed and are, overall, nearly complete fitness regimes—with some important exceptions. Most of the students whom I meet at these conferences have little to no experience of conscious breathing. Breathing is not part of their training for daily fitness, and based on my observation of their nervous systems, this is no surprise.

Meditation, or sitting in stillness, is also something that is widely left out of the fitness world. I believe that it is due to the lack of conscious breathing work. As a result, students retain the emotional blockages or issues they had when they began their fitness lifestyles. For example, Sally, a thirty-year-old woman who began her cutting-edge fitness program because she was suffering from a stressful life, had chronic digestion issues and trouble sleeping. She also needed to take antianxiety pills to function in her career and congested city environment. One year after practicing her new fitness program, Sally was thinner, leaner, much stronger, and more flexible, and she had notably more energy throughout the day. But she still had her digestive problems, sleep disorder, and anxiety issues. Those had not changed. One of the reasons was that even though her workout had many positive benefits, Sally worked out so intensely that her fight-or-flight response remained triggered most of the time. She worked out as if she was going into battle. She also has not learned any kind of meaningful breathing exercises, so her imbalanced nervous system was not given an opportunity to rebalance itself. It was almost like she was putting her emotions into a pressure cooker. At the end of her workout, she did not sit in meditation to center her mind and ground her; instead, she headed to the showers and started scrolling through her text messages. Although Sally's workout has achieved some of her goals and has contributed to her functioning at a new level in her life, the cause of her relationship challenges and unhappiness had gone virtually unchanged. This example of Sally is what I commonly see coming from the high-level fitness world—people who are strong, flexible, aerobically developed, but generally unhappy, tense, and anxious. A great many of them have so much unresolved grief and anger inside that upon experiencing their first breathing workshop with me, they have a powerful release of deeply suppressed emotions. By the end of the workshop, the tears are flowing freely, and many report that the tears continue to fall off and on for a day or two. Of course, not only do feelings come up, but because their feelings and memories rise up above the horizon, they are able to learn something about themselves and their relationships that they did not know two hours earlier. This, of course, is quite a stunning experience to many. After seeing how simple yet powerful the work is, how accessible this rapid and positive change can be for them, they cannot believe that it is not widely taught. Some even become angry that they have not been offered these simple techniques before.

Now, the limitations that I have spoken of here are not only in the fitness world, they are unfortunately also readily found in the yoga world. Some just flail their anguish-ridden bodies to and fro for an hour and a half, knowing that they will feel somewhat better at the end of class, gasping for breath occasionally. In my travels from city to city, students constantly tell me that quality breathing is not commonly taught in their areas and that most yoga classes they have attended are not breath-centric. For example, when I present my work at yoga conferences, sometimes there are two hundred or more workshops offered, but only two or three of them are dedicated to breathing. Breathing work and breath-initiated movement in the yoga world are still young, but they are beginning to grow, and there are some fine teachers involved in spreading the knowledge.

A DAILY PRACTICE TO CHANGE YOUR LIFE

Breath-initiated movement is the term that is used to describe movement that is initiated and guided by conscious breathing (remember, conscious breathing is deciding to breathe a certain way, not autopilot breathing), where each inhale and exhale sets into motion a movement. You generally move slowly, and you do not move without your breath leading the way. Practicing any movement regime in this way offers much more than the typical workout because while you are creating a healthy body, you are also calming the chaotic, throbbing storm in the mind, the relentless critical noise and drama that can feel like your own private purgatory. Breath-initiated movement purposefully and directly eliminates this. Then, when your mind and nervous system are calm, you see life differently. It is a simple process, but simple things appear otherwise when there is an absence of knowledge. I have observed it positively impact thousands of lives, mentally, emotionally, and physically. Breath-initiated movement does not just open your muscles and joints, it opens your eyes, and you see the world through these new eyes.

Hatha yoga and qigong are both powerful systems of breath-initiated movement, but there are other wonderful regimes as well, such as tai chi and other effective Western variations and interdisciplinary hybrids. Whatever discipline you choose, your practice should include breath-led strength building and stretching as well as meditation or mental stillness exercises to accelerate your transformation. If you practice at least one hour a day, the accumulative effect will heal, empower, and illuminate.

- Breathing heals the emotional body. It dispels emotional pain and accumulated stress, cultivating a peaceful mind and body.
- Meditation illuminates. It trains your mind to focus and recalibrates the nervous system. With the tornado mind subdued, the inner voice of your higher mind and conscience can be finally heard and followed.
- Conscious movement empowers. Led by conscious breathing, conscious movement removes stress and emotional pain from the body that often manifest as tightness and/or physical pain and even some illness. This initiates physical healing.

The health benefits are almost too numerous to list because breath-initiated movement is a holistic practice. This means that the benefits are partly provided by targeting specific objectives, but unexpected benefits also occur. Sometimes a human being should be treated by focusing on a certain part or damaged area of that person. For example, a broken leg should be physically reset and immobilized with a plaster cast, and pain relievers should be given to the injured person for a few days. Healing as an overall holistic art is not approached by targeting the collection of parts but, instead, by understanding that we function as a whole system and that our functioning cannot be fully comprehended solely in terms of our component parts. This is seen in almost any sport, as we focus on one objective but receive other benefits. For example, many people play golf because they love the game itself, but the player also receives benefits from walking outdoors surrounded by trees and grass and breathing fresh air, as well as socializing without using technological devices. The aggregate healing benefits of breath-initiated movement are due to the synergistic power of the parts affecting one another. This kind of physical regime reshapes your life, not just your body. To develop this kind of practice, we need to set aside time for it rather than squeeze it into our lives.

After years of practicing within several yoga disciplines, I found that some were more healing to the outer body and some to the emotional body. What I wanted was a complete practice that would do both, a truly balanced practice. I decided to coalesce the most powerful tools that I had learned from the different disciplines I had studied. I began coalescing breath-centric vinyasa yoga and therapeutic yoga as well as the energy direction and joint-healing work of qigong. The positive results in my life were dramatic. When I introduced them into the yoga room as a teacher, I saw powerful transformations begin to occur in people's lives. Over the years, I have continually refined this hybrid practice to where it is now and share it with people across the world. I enjoy working with people of all ages and from all walks of life and points of view—agnostics, the spiritual, and the religious. This work is for everyone who wants a balanced holistic practice that is both safe and transformative.

Where Will You Find the Time?

I know that you are likely to say, "Where do I find the time to practice for an hour a day? I don't have enough time to do anything now." How much time do you spend playing video games? How much time do you spend on social media? How much time do you spend reading the sports page? Too many people know more about their favorite quarterback then about themselves. Do a personal cost-benefit analysis on passive activities, such as watching sports or TV shows, or playing video games. In order to fulfill your highest calling in this life and find a deeper kind of happiness, you may have to give up or at least cut back on the time you spend on passive entertainment. Do a cost-benefit analysis. You'll find the time.

CREATE A CREED

A creed in this context is a personal codification of your life intention and what you stand for. To create a recitation of your intention of life is a powerful practice. Most religions include a daily prayer to recite, such as the Lord's Prayer or Islam's Salat. It is practiced in almost every religion and also in some of the most elite military brotherhoods such as the United States Special Forces. It is utilized by both religions and military brotherhoods because it works. The Special Forces would never consider employing such a ritual if it were not effective. They have no time or concern for superficial rituals; they recite their creed every morning for one reason only—it is effective. Reciting our creed triggers not only our mental faculties and not only our intention but also the astounding power of our imagination to create that which we envision. As part of your new practice, I strongly recommend that you think carefully and create or choose a creed that will become the manifesto of your life's work and repeat it each and every morning. It can be totally original or something that you already adhere to. Make it your own. It need not be lengthy, even a simple motto with which you resonate is enough. If you consider yourself a spiritual person, use a creed that moves you deeply, or again, write your own. If you consider yourself neither religious nor spiritual but agnostic with your own vision of life, write your own creed and live by it as if it were your religion.

Here is a wonderful example of a prayer written by American theologian Reinhold Niebuhr. It is well known as the Serenity Prayer and has been adopted by Alcoholics Anonymous and other twelve-step programs. This simple yet profound prayer could of itself be someone's creed.

> *God, grant me the serenity to accept the things I cannot change, the courage to change the things I can, and the wisdom to know the difference.*

With some minor rewording, this could also be adopted by an agnostic. Over the years, you may find the desire to rework or even create a new creed as you go through life changes. Remember that a creed is a living, breathing thing and not a fossil.

Here is of a creed of my own.

> *We are those who love God as God is—without needing to impose a human personality or face upon it/him/her. We move through the world as an ally to humankind, aiming to be a harmonious power in a disharmonious world. Amidst an environment of gossip and negativity, we will offer inspiration and grace. In a noisy, hurried place, we will provide calm. In a fearful place, we will provide courage and inspiration. In a place of decay, we will help rebuild. And in all instances, with humility, we will influence or even lead by example. Following our inner voice, we attain a level of beingness that is apparent to those who have eyes to see, so, like sitting in the presence of a calm stream in a forest, a person will want to stop and sit beside us and, feeling better because of it, will ruminate on improving his or her own life.*

ABOVE THE HORIZON

The principle breathing practice we utilize during movement and postures is commonly called Ujjayi breathing in yoga communities. I call it ocean breathing because it sounds like the ebb and flow of the ocean waves, and so the phrase itself reminds a student how to make the breath sound. This form of breathing is critical to our practice as it heals and energizes the body, harmonizes the nervous system, and heals and enlivens the spirit. In other words, ocean breathing is the keystone of our posture and movement practice. The breath is focused in the lower throat and sounds like the ocean surf or the wind through leaves. One of the central purposes for this technique of making the ocean sound is that it partially closes the air passage so that the breath can be regulated for both the inhaling and the exhaling. When we inhale, we do so deeply into the entire chest area, focusing particularly on expanding the side ribs out toward our elbows, and then we exhale from our lower belly up. When we exhale this way, the chest naturally contracts toward the center of the torso as the lungs deflate. We breathe in and out of the nose. When I teach the ocean breathing technique, I always direct students to begin with the mouth wide open, as if saying, "Ahhh . . ."

This sound should be made not only during exhaling but also during inhaling. Once the technique of making the sound of the ocean is memorized, then we proceed to breathe in exactly the same way, but with the mouth closed.

Ocean breathing is best learned from a competent teacher. If a teacher is not available in your area, I have a DVD available online, entitled *Learn to Breathe*, to heal yourself and your relationships. But nothing replaces the eyes, ears, and experience of a good teacher standing next to you.

The combination of conscious breathing and movement can refresh your tired body far better than a cup of coffee without the crash in energy later in the day. Many, including myself, find that breath-initiated movement stimulates creativity. I have seen many people stop their practice to write down their sudden burst of inspiration. In fact, many yoga teachers offer yoga-and-writing seminars or yoga-and-art courses because of this well-known benefit of inspiration. Even more significant is that regulated breathing and movement can trigger old memories, bringing hidden details of those memories and their corresponding emotions up to the surface.

This is very healing and can be the catalyst of an emotional logjam being swept away, allowing desperately needed change to occur spontaneously within you. When this happens and a pocket of grief is released, it transmutes that grief into inspiration and sometimes even joy, and it transforms long-term anger into a place where forgiveness is finally possible.

For example, when grief, shame, or anger are suppressed, although you may be aware that you have submerged feelings from years gone by, you may not be able to process them, because they have been suppressed for so long. They can be almost unidentifiable. Through short periods of stronger breath work, your emotions can be lifted up above the horizon. Once they are above the horizon, you can see them clearly and begin to understand and put your feelings into context. When you begin to understand and process your feelings, you cease to be afraid of them. Once unafraid of your feelings, you can begin to heal. Once you heal, then you become a more integrated and actualized person, and your relationships become healthier and more vital. Powerful breathing exercises have been incorporated into some forms of psychotherapy because of this very aspect of revealing suppressed emotions or trauma.

Exercise:

Practice ocean breathing whenever you can. Try it for five minutes before you speak to someone challenging on the phone, while stuck in traffic, while cooking a time-sensitive meal, or while performing a simple but tedious task like shoveling snow. This will enable you to deal with your challenges in a superior way. The challenges may not change, but you'll change, and so the outcome may change.

ABOUT HATHA YOGA

We have had holistic technologies to transform us for thousands of years, technologies such as hatha yoga, qigong, tai chi, etc. Personally, I practice and teach a carefully designed qigong-influenced hatha yoga because it transformed my life. I have since witnessed it transform tens of thousands of lives mentally, emotionally, and physically. When your mind and nervous system are calm, you think differently. Hatha yoga does not just open your muscles and joints, it opens your eyes, and you see the world through these new eyes.

Hatha yoga was born within the Hindu culture of India and, therefore, is often seen as irrevocably imbedded within the Hindu religion. But because the human soul transcends man-made religions and cultures, hatha yoga is ultimately a transformational path that is non-dogmatic. Hatha yoga is not exclusive to one religion and is inclusive of all religions. Yoga is also practiced by agnostics and atheists with equal benefit. Put simply, one could say hatha yoga is an ancient and powerful method of self-transformation that utilizes crystal-clear mental focus and deep breathing while performing a series of special postures. Although, to the outside observer, hatha yoga appears to be primarily physical, its benefits are far reaching. I consider it an essential art.

FINDING THE RIGHT STYLE OR TEACHER FOR YOU

To quote Buddha, "Believe nothing, no matter where you read it, or who said it, no matter if I have said it, unless it agrees with your own reason and your own common sense." Because of the enormous popularity of hatha yoga today, there are so many styles that trying to figure out what style is best for you can seem exhausting, but with a little patience you will find the right teacher for your needs. Just like finding a good doctor or dentist, rely on referrals. Find out from the people you respect most who they are practicing with. Yoga today has some of the same problems in leadership that can be found elsewhere, where the charismatic leader of a movement portrays a theatrical, mystical variation of himself or herself to the public, and that persona is regarded by the movement's followers as genuine. Like in *The Wizard of Oz*, we are asked to pay no attention to the man behind the curtain. Sometimes the leaders of healing movements are seduced and overwhelmed with fame and forget that they are educators and not celebrities. There is an old saying, "Fame is never a blessing from God." It is the same problem that notoriously occurs in religious communities. I believe it is partly because there is no governing body that supervises the behavior or the psychological development of the teachers. There are, of course, arguments to both sides of this problem. Many believe that without a guiding governing body of ethics and behavior, this problem will just worsen over time. The other side of the argument is that if a governing body is created to oversee and supervise ethics, then who is going to govern the governing body? This familiar issue constantly rears its head, especially in religion and politics.

Recommended criterion to finding a sane, safe, and inspiring yoga or qigong teacher:

- The essential environment of a class should be welcoming, unifying, respectful, and safe.
- Avoid working with teachers who often draw attention to themselves rather than to the practice.
- Avoid those who are not kind, who shame or scold, or who sexualize themselves or their students.
- Avoid teachers who teach their postures in only one way and expect people of all levels of fitness to accomplish them.
- Avoid those who bluntly impose their religious or spiritual views upon you.
- Avoid teachers who are habitually late to their own classes.

What is incumbent upon you are four things:

1. You must inform the teacher of any pre-existing injury that could be reinjured through a movement-based regime—for example, chronic back pain, a damaged knee, tennis elbow, or a recent surgery. Also, if you have not been physically active for a long period of time, you should not expect your body to suddenly be the way it used to be. Inform your teacher that you have not been active and that you want to go very slow to prevent injury. Sharing basic information like this with your

teacher will help her or him to help you avoid reinjury. This is key to a safe practice. Just take a moment to wave the teacher over and whisper privately what your conditions are, including pregnancy. There is no need for the rest of the class to overhear this. This is good reason to arrive a little bit early to class so that you can speak with the teacher in advance of the class start time. A good teacher will listen carefully and give you alternative poses to do.

2. You need to observe if the teacher tends to physically push his or her students deeper into postures, and make sure this does not happen to you. If this occurs, it means you will probably have to go to a different teacher. This is particularly important with forward bends. Being pushed deeper into a forward bend can cause a spinal injury or tearing of the hamstrings. Well meaning as the teacher probably is, many people have been injured in this way. I am not saying that a teacher cannot help you immensely with some physical contact that guides and informs, but contact is not the same as pushing/forcing you deeper into a posture. Never be afraid to speak up and ask a teacher to stop if he or she is adjusting you in any way that does not feel right to your body. It is your body, and you have to live in it for the rest of your life; the teacher does not.

3. Follow your intuition in regard to safety. If a teacher demonstrates a posture that you feel will be too intense for you, you are most likely right. Never do anything that you feel is unsafe.

4. Avoid practicing with a forceful intention. Extreme effort is quite often counterproductive in a health regime like this. Extreme stretching will very likely cause injuries. Practiced wisely, a breath-initiated movement regime should help to

heal many injuries and not create new ones. Remember, forcing your way through life and ignoring the signals of your body may be the reason why you have created your health issues to begin with.

Be aware that some yoga teachers are very attached to various traditions of yoga. It is important that you know there is not only one yoga tradition; there are many, and there is much discrepancy and sometimes even strong disagreement between them—just like the squabbling in the medical world, religious world, and political world. Be careful not to adopt methods solely on the fact that they are said or believed to come from a tradition. Question everything.

I personally have not found that tradition alone guarantees authenticity or richness of teaching. There are plenty of world famous (now infamous) teachers and religious leaders who followed tradition to the letter and whose credentials were impeccable but their actions ultimately were not. To quote American theologian and ethicist Reinhold Niebuhr, "We are admonished in Scripture to judge men by their fruits, not by their roots; and their fruits are their character, their deeds, and accomplishments." In fact, many of the great spiritual leaders throughout history were rebels against the tradition of their times. Jesus of Nazareth rejected the Mosaic Law. Buddha rejected the Hindu priesthood. Mohammed rejected the desert religions of his region and created something new. It seems that today's traditionalists worship yesterday's nontraditionalists.

I recommend wise and cautious adherence to the way you are taught the form of your practice. Adherence of form has its value and credence in the beginning. Once you become adept at a process, each day you will find personal subtleties and should adjust to what is appropriate for you at that moment. To me, to adhere to formality indefinitely fossilizes the process, and then it is no longer a living process.

If you find that hatha yoga is not the right fit for you, particularly on the philosophical side, there are other health regimes similar to hatha yoga that can be found within Sufism, Buddhism, Taoism, traditional Chinese medicine, and so on. Christianity-influenced yoga is now more readily available as well. Whatever your worldview is, your philosophy of life or creed, I strongly recommend that you incorporate it into your breath-initiated practice, your Lifelong Fitness regime.

ABOUT QIGONG

Qigong was born within the culture of ancient China and in my view is the fraternal twin of hatha yoga. While most of the breathing practices that I have seen in hatha yoga are done seated, some are done while standing. In qigong, it is the opposite. With some exceptions, most of the breathing exercises are done standing. Qigong has some qualities and techniques that are not commonly found in yoga that I find very valuable to include when building a holistic practice. For example, in regard to the primary joints, the shoulders and hips, most of the movements in hatha yoga are done in a linear fashion, whereas in qigong many movements are done in a circular or even figure-eight fashion. Since the shoulder and hip joints are designed for multidirectional movement, I think it is of significant importance to keep them healthy, limber, and articulate. Another notable and powerful part of qigong is that once you become adept, you can not only feel the life force, or Qi, moving through the body but you can actually learn to follow it as if listening to a guiding voice. Though it is a wordless voice, it is a guide nonetheless. You follow the power of the Qi, and when you follow this power, you move spontaneously, fluidly, and beautifully and feel overtaken in a most wonderful sense. Of course, to do it you need to turn off the cerebral mind and listen in a new way. Students are often shocked by the experience of turning off the intellect for a time and that your awareness is actually heightened. This is because the cerebral mind is allowed to rest and recenter itself. It is, in a way, like hitting the refresh button on your computer. Qigong is learned by memorizing various forms or patterns of movement led by the breath. After some weeks or months of practice, you begin to learn to feel the movement of your life force coursing through the energy channels of your body. This becomes more vivid over time, and some point you begin to feel this immediately upon practicing and feel it more and more as you breathe and move. When your practice is complete, you have a great sense of lightness, as if your body were not made of flesh and bone but of vibrating energy. When you walk away from your practice area, you feel an amazing sense of renewal, vibrancy, and centeredness. Once you have experienced this feeling again and again, there is no longer any doubt that a life force courses through your body and being. Some call it Qi, or Ki, or Chi, or Prana; some call it nothing and simply smile.

One of the wonderful and practical aspects of this practice is that you do not need any special clothing or equipment or special location. Qigong can be done wearing any kind of loose-fitting clothing and shoes and socks. So you can do this, potentially, in an office setting, in a park, or on your lawn in the sunshine. And this extreme portability of the practice offers you opportunities to practice whenever you have a few minutes of free time. This allows the opportunity to transform five minutes of standing around into five minutes of practice. For example, on your way to an important meeting that is causing you some stress, you could park your car and then practice for a few minutes in the parking lot to calm down. Then when you enter the meeting room, you will have a renewed calm and power that you would not have had by habitually dwelling on your thoughts and worry. I recommend that when you practice qigong you practice in slow motion, as slowly as you can. This will bring greater intelligence and facility to your body. Many of the high-level martial arts are practiced at very slow speed, what we call slow motion. This is a critical way of teaching the body micromovements and microadjustments. But when a martial artist finally does have to move at high speeds, he or she can move so fast that you can barely track the movement. It is like trying to watch a catfight; all you see is a blur. This is one of the ways that our reflexes are enhanced through our breath-initiated movement, and just like with the other types of slow-motion movement, the nervous system is triggered to rest and digest. The main limitation that I have found with qigong is that as life enhancing and health enhancing as it is, it does not seem to have the same intense emotional transforming power that some hatha yoga breathing practices offer. I think this is because hatha yoga postures dramatically open the body, stretching muscles and opening the energy channels while you breathe powerfully, expanding and contracting the chest. This seems to purge cumulative negative emotion much more quickly and intensely. This is a key technique for transforming on the psychological level, freeing us from stifling neuroses and addictions, and by illuminating our blind spots. Qigong is known for cultivating health and longevity, but to my knowledge it is not well known for rapid psychological or emotional transformation.

Qigong is defined basically as life-force cultivation. Pranayama is defined basically as the extension of the life force. In other words, they mean almost the exact same thing. They are two traditions from two different cultures that have the same end in mind, as well as many similar (and in some cases identical) techniques.

Intention is more powerful than action;
breath is more powerful than movement.
Set your intention and breathe—then
move and watch your movement soar
and your life flourish.

THE PRACTICE OF MENTAL STILLNESS

We cannot rest when we are constantly running away from something or running after something. Running must stop. We must allow the body to rest; we must allow our emotions to rest and the mind to take silence. We need a new kind of awareness—more powerful and more subtle. Then we can fall into a state where we can witness ourselves minus the guilt, shame, and frustration. Just our own being, naked. Then we become more human-like in the higher sense.

I saw an article title recently: "Controlling a robot with your mind." How about controlling yourself with your mind? Even your own tongue with your mind? As the storm in your mind rages, it causes you to become obsessed with your life challenges, and you become more and more self-centered. As the storm batters your mind, the noise drowns out the voices of intuition and conscience. These are the voices that would guide you with wisdom through this life, and without them you are like a rudderless ship. Due to this, you make your decisions based on logic some of the time, but most of the time you are compelled by negative emotions, compulsions, and fear. This reminds me of an old film in which an immense tornado was tearing through the Midwest and a family of farmers barely managed to make their way into their storm cellar. Once inside, the family tried to make contact with neighbors on their short-wave radio, but because of the electrical force of the tornado, all communication with the outside world was cut off. Even if they did manage to get reception, it would've been drowned out by the deafening cacophony. All they could do was hunker down in their shelter as the tornado ravaged their world above; their sole focus was survival. Eventually, the tornado passed by, and then they heard, at last, static transmissions echoing from the radio, and the family could once again communicate with the outside world. This analogy is quite descriptive of how we are when paralyzed by a tornado in our own minds—our only concern is for ourselves and our immediate family, and we lose empathy for others. We are too busy, stressed, and overwhelmed to sign a petition, or hand a dollar to an old woman on the street, or join a noble cause. But the difference here is that we are creators of our own tornado. So, that means we can un-create it. When we do, we can at last hear the echoing transmissions from within that were there all the time but our drama had drowned out the voices of our intuition and conscience.

We are fraught with turmoil partly because of the onslaught of external forces but mostly because we do not know techniques to reharmonize ourselves. Teaching your mind to become quiescent (still, quiet, or inactive) will make you more emotionally stable and less reactive. Your natural daytime state is alert stillness, so to relearn how to be this way is not as difficult as you might imagine. To the novice, there is an assumption that when the mind completely comes to a resting state and is inactive, we will ether fall into sleep or die, but in fact a quiescent mind means that your "inner bean-counter" has stopped counting, sorting, deciding, and criticizing. Your inner calculator, cash register, and PDA are all silent. When you find yourself in this state, you discover something amazing—you are still awake, you are still alert, and you are still totally aware of your surroundings. But you are tranquil, free from disturbing emotions, and free from craving. This is the state of beingness that you have heard of or read about, and it can be overwhelmingly beautiful. As many teachers have pointed out, we are called human *beings*. As previously mentioned, our inner state can also be affected or even controlled by conscious practices. Meditation is one tool to help us achieve this. Yet, so many people have tried to meditate and found the experience frustrating and fruitless. I think this may be because so many meditation teachers are using the right methods with the wrong people, or the wrong methods with the right people. For example, if I were teaching swimming and someone came to me and said, "Max, I want you to teach me to swim, but you need to know that I am terrified of the water," I am not going to teach this person in the same way I would teach my other students. Instead, I would take him or her to the shallow end, to the very beginning so that this person may achieve some success and grow to trust the process. Similarly, with meditation we must use the best techniques for people who are under great stress and turmoil. If someone comes to me and says, "Max, I want to learn to still my mind, but you need to know that I am in turmoil most of time, and I feel a lot of anxiety," I am not going to ask that student to sit down on the floor, close his eyes, and think of nothing—because it is likely that he will fail, and this is normal. So, I will use a different technique, with which he will succeed. Then in the future, I may ask him to quiet his mind and empty it of all thoughts. So, the technique we will begin with is a conscious practice that uses your imagination and will help you to convert your tornado mind into a tranquil mind.

Stillness exercises:

The human imagination is unfathomably powerful and even mysterious in its far-reaching capacity. We all use our imagination daily for creative projects, fantasy, and in entertainment (from the stimulation of other people's imaginations) mainly via television shows, films, and novels. But our imagination can also be utilized to change our inner state. To do this stillness exercise, you will need these things:

- A quiet space
- A straight-back chair or cushion to sit on the floor
- A trusted and sincere friend with a nice speaking voice to read aloud to you

Sit in a comfortable upright position with closed eyes, and when you are ready, have your friend read this next section out loud. I have included parenthetical notes for the reader to indicate pauses. Reader, read slowly, with a soft voice (take your time).

Reader Begins Here

Close your eyes. Lift your spine toward the ceiling, and at the same time, relax your shoulders.

(pause)

Relax the jaw while you keep your spine tall.

(pause)

Relax your eyes.

(pause)

Now, begin breathing and count your breaths. See if you can stay focused on your breath, and count them for two minutes.

(after 2 minutes)

Now, bring your whole attention into your chest—your heart center—and allow it to soften.

(pause)

It will soften because the heart's natural state is to be relaxed.

(pause)

Now I invite you to use your imagination.

(pause)

As you sit with your eyes closed, imagine someone has brought to you a small, eight-year-old girl from a village in a war-torn country. She is sitting just in front of you—only three feet away.

(pause)

For her entire short life, this little girl has been surrounded by violence, grief, anger, fear, and pain. And she has not known anyone who is not afraid, in grief, or angry.

(pause)

But today someone has brought this little girl to you because the person knows of you as being a peaceful person, and he or she wants this girl to experience being in the presence of someone who is peaceful and unafraid.

(pause)

She has heard that there is a practice of peace, and she very much wants to learn. She is sitting and watching you with the hope that she can learn something from you that will make her feel better and something that she can take back to her village to teach the other children. This little girl is now in front of you. She is trying to learn by copying you.

(pause)

She is sitting exactly the way you are sitting. So make certain that you are sitting in the position that you want her to memorize. Make any adjustments you would like to your sitting position now.

(pause)

What about your hand position? Do you want her to memorize this position? Because whatever you are doing, she will memorize it and teach the other children.

(pause)

The way you place your hands, she places her hands. The hands are an extension of the mind. To relax your mind, relax your hands. And what about your face? Is it truly relaxed? Or is your face holding tension in the same places that it usually holds tension? See if you can relax every muscle in your face now.

(pause)

You do not have to have a smile on your face, but perhaps you could have the seed of a smile.

(pause)

Sit just as you want this little girl to sit—tall, strong, open, and peaceful. She is learning to be in peace by watching the example you set.

(pause)

Now what about your breathing? Make sure that your breath is loud enough so that she can hear it. She has heard of this breath of peace, so make sure she can hear it.

(pause)

Good.

(pause)

Now she has closed her eyes. She is sitting just like you. Her breathing sounds exactly like yours. And she is beginning to feel more peaceful, and unafraid—for the first time.

(pause)

You sit together, in peace, and strength, and solidarity.

(pause 30 seconds)

Good. Now, when you are ready, slowly open your eyes.

At first glance you may surmise that this is a visualization, but you would be only partly correct. This exercise asks you to do more than visualize; it also requires you to sense your body posture and degrees of muscle and skin relaxation and activation. It even has you breathe consciously, not just visualize it.

This exercise often brings up a great deal of emotion. My students often wipe tears from their face upon completion because it puts the practice of relaxing into a different category. It is so easy to see value in the context of this child, easier than it is for our own life. When I lead a group of people through this practice, I keep my eyes open and observe them. What I see is the group will sit with far superior posture, with much more relaxed faces and more conscious hand positions. They remember to breathe the entire time, and their postures never falter. And most important, they achieve the state that they want this little girl to attain. It is from their compassion for her that they are motivated to take their stillness exercise to a new level. And this works on virtually everyone, everywhere I go. It is incredibly beautiful to witness. Our personal imagination will provide archetypes that are meaningful to us.

The actual archetypes that you use are symbols and are valuable only in their ability to direct your energies. Few understand that what happens in your mind is much more important than the symbols that your mind uses.

Recently, I received the following thank-you note regarding this very exercise. I am sharing it with you now to elucidate the far-reaching effects of work like this.

Max, I have to tell you that the meditation you led us through, about the seven-year-old girl, has really made an impact on my everyday life. I imagine she is with me in the mornings when I'm getting my six-year-old daughter ready for school. This time of the day used to be very stressful for us because it's so early and my daughter doesn't move too quickly. I try to be very mindful in my words and actions so that I can be an example of how to get through the morning with loving kindness. Now, this time is no longer stressful, but peaceful and enjoyable. Thank you for teaching me this.

~ A student

I recommend that you regularly use your imagination to help you with your practice of stillness and meditation. At some point in the future, you will not need to do this in order to quiet your mind, but until then, use this technique freely. Here is another simple visualization exercise that you can do to learn to relax into stillness and even to heal. This exercise is ideal to do at the end of your breath-initiated movements practice.

You will need these things:

- A quiet space to lie down. It should be warm and comfortable.
- A trusted and sincere friend to read aloud to you.

Make yourself as comfortable as you can on your back, close your eyes, and when you are ready, have your friend read this next section out loud with a soft and kind voice.

Reader Begins Here

Make yourself as comfortable as you can on your back, and just rest and deeply relax.

(pause)

Breathe deeply and in a relaxed way.

(pause)

Relax the jaw and the eyes.

(pause)

Now I invite you to use your imagination . . . and step out of your own body.

(pause)

Step up out of your own body and look down upon it . . . now, reach toward and adjust your body as if you were a great healer.

(pause)

Adjust the shoulders.

(pause)

Look at the face. See if there are any hints of sadness or anger left on the face. Perhaps lightly touch the face with your fingertips, smoothing the lines away.

(pause)

Now scan the rest of the body. Find any area that is holding sadness in.

(pause)

Reach into the body, find the sadness, and pull it out. Just throw it away.

(pause)

Let the pain leave your hands.

(pause)

The body you are observing should be softer and more open now, more restful. Lay both of your hands on the heart center of the body below you.

(pause)

Send golden light out in a stream from your radiant heart—through your hands and into the heart below . . . healing it.

(pause)

Now, climb back into this newly healed body below you. Once you are united with your body, relax into this body, feel the familiar form, pleasantly aware that it has been healed and so feels more at ease. Now, focus on your own radiant heart center and expand; you are the light of your heart beyond your body.

(pause)

Envision your heart being so bright that it helps people sense their own heart centers.

(pause)

Your heart leads hundreds, thousands of people to heal their own hearts, to remember their own true nature…

End Session

It is by teaching your intellect to become quiet when you want it to be quiet that you can become happier, more present for others, and more open to the joy of the present moment.

Exercises to Calm the Tornado Mind

- When you feel in turmoil, remember that the turmoil is a symptom and not who you are. You have the power to calm the mind—first by knowing that you can and then by deciding to do it.
- Close your eyes and take a huge, slow breath into your chest, expanding the ribs to the sides and then exhaling slowly. Repeat for at least two minutes.

- Focus on what you have and your gratitude for it. For example, perhaps you read bad news in the newspaper, but you still have eyes to read with, hands to hold the paper with, and the time to sit and read the paper. When we refocus and appreciate what we have, we tend not to be reactive to negative circumstances.
- If you know how to meditate, sit for a minimum of ten minutes every morning or evening.

MAKE ROOM IN YOUR LIFE FOR YOUR PRACTICE

Once you are committed to a daily practice of six days a week, there is the practical concern of where to do it. I strongly recommend that you work under the supervision of a qualified and inspiring teacher for at least one year. Only after practicing regularly for at least six months should you consider practicing at home on occasion without the guidance of a teacher. The reason for this is that unless a person is a professional movement specialist, such as a high-level dancer or martial artist, most of us have very limited body awareness and proprioception. The level of body awareness of the average person who does not have a physical discipline of some kind is quite low from my observation. Most of us tend to only be familiar with the front of our bodies and know very little about the sides or the back of the body. So trying to learn specific movements from a book, or even a DVD, is not advisable. You will think that you are doing exactly what you see, but this is rarely the case. For the sake of injury prevention and the highest quality experience, work with a teacher who can guide you gradually over time. I practiced six days a week for about two years before I took my practice into my home. Then I would practice between home and the yoga studio about every other day. Do not misunderstand: You will not be complete in your abilities after one year. You will continue to improve year after year under the guidance of an adept teacher. Even if you do decide to bring your practice into your home, please continue to work with a teacher perhaps one or two days a week for many years to come.

Now, for your home practice, you must create a quality space for your breath-initiated movement, even if that means you need to permanently clear out some of your furniture to make an empty space in your living room. It may not be the best-decorated choice, but it may be the best health choice of your life. To make space in your physical world for your three imperatives makes a powerful statement to yourself and to the world of your new priorities and intention. So many households now have a media room, but if that flat screen TV has not made you happy and healthy by now, it is probably not going to. As entertaining as it is, it will probably have no positive impact on your relationships, your health, or your transformation. But creating a room, or at least a designated space to practice the three imperatives will change your life. I remember quite clearly when I committed to my practice and cleared out a quarter of the space in my living room. It looked a bit empty when I was not practicing, but it felt like the fullest space in my home. It held my resolve, my intention, my healing. To me it made the statement that my world began with my practice and ended with my practice. I was not going to simply squeeze my practice into my daily life; it was now going to be the center of my life. That empty space became a sacred space to me.

Try not to make this a dual-use space. Keep it just for practice. It should be absolutely clean and free of dust. No clutter, no random pieces of art; have nothing on the walls or on the floor that does not add to your experience. If at all possible, air out the room prior to practicing. If the weather is nice, open the windows so that you can breathe fresh, clean air. Air quality is highly significant and one of the most overlooked aspects of our health.

CREATING A PERSONAL ALTAR

Altars have long been used as a focal point in spiritual rituals for a reason. Creating a personal altar in our homes is very conducive as a profound reminder of what is important to us. An altar does not have to be religious. If you are religious, you can certainly make it so, using icons or images that evoke feelings of serenity and strength from your faith. If you are not religious, the altar can still be an extremely powerful personal reminder. It can be a focal point of images and archetypes that are meaningful to you, or people or places that inspire and evoke the best in you. This could be as simple as photographs of your family. If you look at the desks of many business people, they essentially have a small altar to their families, an array of photographs placed so that they can be reminded throughout the day why they work so hard. Besides photographs of your family, you might consider images of inspirational people in your life or exemplary people whom you have studied and who bring out the best in you. These people do not have to be thought of as gurus or saints, or people above you, just as people who inspire your own best qualities.

Your altar could have a token or a memento of a special trip or walk in nature, such as a stone or a shell—something that reminds you of a moment when you felt whole and happy. You can include the photo of a beloved pet. There are no wrong choices. Your altar is yours and can be as simple or as elaborate as is helpful to you. It can be a continuous artwork in progress, a creative expression to enjoy. Add to it, remove things, reorganize the placement. Keep it a living and fluid gathering of symbols that speak to you. If you leave it unchanged, your mind is likely to not really see it after a while. By making small changes frequently, you will tend to notice it more, thereby increasing its impact. An altar is a powerful addition to your practice space, but you can have it anywhere in your home that you want. The point is to have it in a place that you will see every day and often throughout the day.

A PLACE TO BREATHE

Once you have committed fully to your practice, it is sometimes necessary to overcome obstacles that can thwart your practice. For example, you may not have the money to purchase yoga classes or tai chi classes; you may not have a suitable space to practice. But once committed, you must find a way even when there appears not to be one. After I had been practicing hatha yoga for about three years, I ran into some financial difficulty that caused me to move out of my apartment and into the guest cottage of a good friend. Because I was so short on funds, I had to stop going to the yoga studio where I was practicing six days a week. I could not even afford the monthly tuition any longer, which was heavily discounted. The guest cottage I was staying in was comfortable but small, there was not enough room to do a proper movement-based practice. Spring had just arrived, and the weather was warming up, so I considered practicing outside on my friend's back lawn. But practicing some of the postures on grass is certainly far from ideal, so I searched for a different option. One day I noticed that behind his garage, leaning against the wall, was a full sheet of half-inch thick plywood. It occurred to me that I could use this sheet of plywood as a portable

wooden floor. I could place it on the lawn in the sunshine and practice in the fresh air. After trying this one afternoon, I knew I had
come upon something that was not just a temporary fix but a wonderful new way of practicing. I enjoyed practicing in the outdoors
so much that I actually preferred it to practicing in a studio, as long
as the weather was warm enough. Sometimes I had to wear a lot of
extra clothing, other times I did not, but the air was always fresh,
and the sound of birds singing added to the natural ambience of
my practice. So, if you have a lawn or driveway or porch, you have
a place to practice. If the surface is not made of wood, get a sheet
of plywood. Just a standard 4' x 8' x 0.5" sheet works perfectly. It
may take bit of sandpaper and elbow grease to smooth the surface,
but once you put down your practice mat on the plywood and start
breathing, you will see that it does not matter so much where you
put your mat down, it matters where you are on the inside.

Breathing in Your Car

One of the most neglected areas of our health is giving ourselves
access to clean fresh air when indoors or in a car. There is growing attention given to this recently due to the widespread problem
of allergies, but all should consider changing the air filters in their
homes and offices at least every three months and use the more
expensive, higher quality filters.

Our car, where Americans dwell about two hours per day, is
another place to pay attention to the quality of air circulation. In my
travels, I have observed that the vast majority of people I ride with as
a passenger have no awareness of circulating air in their vehicle. This
includes most taxi drivers. When I ride in the front passenger seat,
I always pay attention to the dashboard controls for air to see how
they are set. Most people have either the AC on in the summer or

the heater on in the winter or nothing on at all. It seems that most drivers are unaware of the third choice, which is air circulation from the outside. I have not yet seen a car that does not have this. You simply turn on the fan control and make sure your vents are open. Fresh air comes into the car—much less complicated than a smartphone. These air vent controls have existed in one form or another for a long time. I have seen air vents on antique cars made as far back as 1930. The result of the widespread neglect of air vents causes people to drive while rebreathing their own stale air for the duration of their commute. After a while, rebreathing stale air can make you feel stressed and slightly claustrophobic, and you are actually denying your body of its critical air source. When this starts to happen, people generally open their windows, but then if it is raining, this is not a practical solution. So, please take a few minutes to examine your dashboard carefully and learn how to bring in fresh air from outside the car without using the AC or heater. If you do, you will feel much better when driving and much more alert.

THE MESSAGE

The message I want to convey to you most of all regarding movement-based exercise is this: Your life is short; if you lose your health, you lose your ability to be active in everything that you now take for granted. You will lose your ability to work, to care for your loved ones, to make love, to walk through nature, to swim, to travel, and to help others. You will lose your ability to sleep through the night and awaken with a smile, to stand and embrace those you love with all your heart. With your health in crisis, almost all of your possessions suddenly mean nothing, and you begin to regret the hours, weeks, and years invested in things that were not important. Every minute you spend in a regime that heals, illuminates, and empowers you deeply serves your family, your loved ones, your work, society at large, and especially your own happiness. To commit to one hour a day of a breath-initiated movement regime will be one of the best investments you could possibly make in this life. Even though I believe that you would best be served by an interdisciplinary practice of hatha yoga and qigong, as I mentioned before there are now multiple interfusion exercise regimes that are intelligently organized and have the potential to be complete practices to adopt for lifelong fitness. If you would take a practice like that and recalibrate it so that each movement is born from your breath and each breath comes from a higher intention, you would have a new kind of practice. Breath-initiated movement can be the engine of any kind of movement that you choose. But your regime must include the intention to deeply relax inside and to not practice as if you are going to war. At the end of your practice, be sure to incorporate a period of absolute rest and stillness for a minimum of seven minutes so that your body can absorb the benefits of the work and learn to be calm. (It's like hitting the *save* button on your computer.) Include a meditation/focus practice into your regime, even if it is only for ten minutes. It is a way of accessing the voice within, your internal GPS, so to speak. A few days a week, your practice should include aerobic activity as well; this can be done by making your movement regime more vigorous for thirty minutes, or you can choose another kind of aerobic exercise. But regardless of what movement you choose, never disassociate from your body but go in the opposite direction toward complete body awareness, breath awareness, and awareness of your highest ideal—all at once. This kind of practice is what will empower your life in a way that you cannot fathom until you are living it. It is not something only for monks somewhere deep in the Himalayas; this work is accessible to each one of us. It is not out of your reach; it is as close to you as your own breath.

THE LONG VIEW

Today, too many of us feel that instead of soaring through our life, we are slogging knee-deep through an uncharted swamp, entangled by economic pressures and political gridlock. We desperately want to find a way out, but our leaders, often myopic and corrupt politicians, keep leading us deeper into the mire. We see the technological world transforming all around us at blistering speed while we ourselves feel stuck in the mud, still trying to fulfill our New Year's resolutions from four years ago. Scientists altruistically keep inventing new ways to repair the damage from humankind's unethical behavior and shortsightedness, but science can only do so much because war, poverty, slavery, and corruption are not tech problems. Science will not make us happy. Biomedicine provides us pills that make us briefly less depressed or less anxious, but when the meds wear off, we find ourselves back where we started—staring right in the mirror wondering, *what do I do now?* Information technology cannot bring meaning into our life, or cause our hearts to brim with gratitude. It cannot give us the courage to shed our skins and become new people. All of these aspects of happiness, fulfillment, and becoming actualized human beings are our individual work and our work alone. To fulfill our potentials and to express and activate our dormant capacities, are a human being's highest aim, and an aim that causes us to be of the greatest service to others. As I have said, we will not see meaningful change in the world without transforming ourselves on a personal level. The good news is that we can do just that. And when enough of us become self-aware, kinder, and truly happy human beings, many of the world's biggest challenges will cease to exist. People who are addicted to entertainment are not likely to want to be interrupted to help others, but people who know the difference between meaningful action and distractive pleasure are more likely to reach out and lend a hand. A self-aware human being has foresight and is more likely to make decisions and to vote based on the common good—not just for today, but also for several generations in the future. Whereas individuals haunted by their past, carrying a lifetime of anger toward their parents or ex-spouse and repeating negative patterns over and over again, are likely to forever seek out ways to numb their unaddressed pain—even being willing to trample over others in the process. It is difficult to feel empathy and emotional generosity when your heart feels like it is trapped in a vise clamp. We owe it to ourselves, to our loved ones, and to our community to heal our past so that we can join them whole and happy.

As the world transitions clumsily to the next phase of human civilization, we can offer leadership and wisdom at this crossroads, pointing the way by example and demanding a more ethical and far-reaching vision of social evolution. To unify is one of the highest forms of leadership.

Speak of principles that you strive to abide by in your own life, and leave out inflammatory words that trigger people to stop listening. There is so much we all have in common. Lead in quiet ways, lead in bold ways, but lead. Our tone of voice and our actions communicate who we are more than what we say, and the quality of how we listen to diverse opinions or ideologies compels people to listen to us. Help people remember who they are and what they are capable of, and when in doubt, just remind them that you respect and care about them.

Both as a society and as individuals we need to practice discernment, to choose wisely as to when we embrace new technology that will enhance our lives, and when we should reject them because they simply do not serve us better. We may even need to be stubborn and work to restore what has served and bound communities together for eons but has been carelessly left behind—treasures like personal interaction, manners, community, and integrity. Remember, everything that is new is not necessarily better.

I have great hope that together we will move from the Age of Entertainment to the Age of Wisdom, with less Facebook friends who are strangers and more face-to-face time with true friends. We have no time for a virtual life. I hope that this book helps you experience the return of the light within your life and feel the embrace of the family that surrounds you. Through self-inquiry and breath-initiated movement, a little bit each day, one breath at a time, we will take the small steps needed to be led out of our own prisons and back into the sunlight where we were born and where our lives are waiting for us.

APPENDIX

STUDENT GUIDELINES FOR A PUBLIC CLASS

These basic guidelines are to help enhance your home practice and experience in public classes as well as aid in creating a collective experience of a sacred personal ritual.

- Practice on an empty stomach. It is recommended that you do not eat at least two hours before movement practice. If a special condition prevents this, eat easily digested foods such as fruit or yogurt one hour before class.
- If possible, bathe prior to your practice. Please do not wear strong scents. This is a courtesy to others, some of whom may have allergies. Also, you may love your perfume or oil, but there will be people who do not, and they may be doing deep breathing two feet away from you.
- Bring no food or beverages into the practice room. If necessary, spring water is okay, but it is recommended to avoid constant sipping. Before and after practice, drink plenty of pure water.
- Bring no shoes into the practice area. In this kind of work, people often put their hands and sometimes their faces on the floor, so please remove your shoes at the door.

- Acquire and use your own practice mat. Using loaner or rental mats is not hygienic.

- Arrive to public classes a few minutes early. Entering class constantly late is very disruptive and disrespectful to others and also to your own nervous system. Consider being prompt as a part of your practice. If you do arrive a few minutes late, take a breath, unravel your mat outside, and then enter as slowly and quietly and as you can. Never enter the studio when the class is in meditation or stillness.

- If you have a preexisting injury or special condition, mention it to the teacher before the start of class so that he or she can help you.

- Absolutely never bring your cell phone into the class. This does not mean turn off the ringer, because sooner or later you will forget. Leave the phone in your car or locker. If you cannot be out of touch for an hour or so, it is indicative of an imbalance in your life. Remember, ninety percent of stress is self-induced.

- Enter the room in silence. Please do not enter and start visiting with others.

- Go right into meditation or stretching. Your practice starts when you walk in.

RECOMMENDED CLOTHING AND CLEANLINESS FOR PUBLIC CLASSES

In short, to participate in a public movement-based class, it is important that you are clean, that you do not smell of body odor or food, and that you are dressed modestly.

WOMEN

Fitted shorts, fitted ankle pants, or capri pants.
Minimal cleavage, if any; wear a bra and underwear.
No jewelry on hands or wrists except commitment rings.

MEN

Wear shorts or fitted ankle pants.
Wear underwear.
Wear a shirt (no muscle tanks).
No adornment or jewelry except commitment rings.

MEN AND WOMEN

Bathe before each class or twice a day.
A towel is good to have handy for sweat management.
Dress modestly as to not sexualize yourself.

Avoid advertisements or logos on clothing. You are not a billboard.

Tie back long hair.

Avoid raw onions and garlic in your diet to prevent body and or breath odor.

FEET AND HANDS

Pedicure; soft skin; clean, short nails.

Treat and heal any athlete's foot.

FOR MORE INFORMATION ON MAX STROM AND HIS MEDIA PRODUCTS

Log on to www.maxstrom.com.